# reality check
# fran cosgrave

# reality check
# fran cosgrave
## my autobiography

Fran Cosgrave
with Martin Roach

JOHN BLAKE

Published by John Blake Publishing Ltd,
3, Bramber Court, 2 Bramber Road,
London W14 9PB, England

www.blake.co.uk

First published in hardback in 2006

ISBN 1 84454 227 0

British Library Cataloguing-in-Publication Data:

A catalogue record for this book is available from the British Library.

Design by www.envydesign.co.uk

Printed and bound in Great Britain by William Clowes Ltd, Beccles, Suffolk

1 3 5 7 9 10 8 6 4 2

Papers used by John Blake Publishing are natural, recyclable products made
from wood grown in sustainable forests. The manufacturing processes conform
to the environmental regulations of the country of origin.

Every attempt has been made to contact the relevant copyright-holders,
but some were unobtainable. We would be grateful if the appropriate people
could contact us.

Photographs p6, 7, 8, 12, 14 © Big Pictures; p9
© Rex Features; p11, 13, 15, 16 © Showbizireland.com;
other pictures from the author's collection.

*For Josh, the brightest star in my life...*
*you make it all worthwhile!*

# ACKNOWLEDGEMENTS

There are so many people to whom I owe thanks for all the good things I've got in my life and, if I've left any of you out, please accept my sincerest apologies.

Mum and Dad, thanks for everything... Gerry and Adam – who could ask for better brothers... I love you both. Tash, you'll always be in my heart. Josh, my beautiful boy who's training to be a Power Ranger and Harry (you're so clever), Maria and George, friends indeed, thank you .

Rachael, Miguel and all the lads... love always. James Spallone... you're a legend. Liam (get a new number) Young, my two amigos Adee and Calum... deadly memories, lads. Gavin R... you're the man. Big shout out to Paul and Jackie... thanks for all those wicked hangovers. Thanks to my man Dave at ASM and to Martin, wordsmith extraordinaire, without whom... Yusef @ Big Bang for spreading the word and Nigel and Toni for getting me to where I'm meant to be. Not forgetting the Westlife boys who turned me into Buzz

Lightyear and the Irish Mafia: Jerry, Ken, Loaf, Finn and Disco Stu... keep on truckin'.

Finally, special thanks to Daisy and Ntalka who believed in me and changed my life

# PROLOGUE

I am 14,000 feet above the Australian jungle, sitting with my feet dangling over the edge of a plane's open door, with Princess Diana's former butler and a famous stand-up comedian right behind me. The air is freezing cold and the noise of the plane's engine drowns out almost all conversation.

I could be totally alone.

I wasn't meant to be here. I am not a celebrity, but everyone else on this lunatic adventure is. I am a nightclub owner, a former bodyguard, a doorman and, sometimes in my thoughts, just a skinny kid from somewhere near Dublin who never felt part of the in-crowd. There have been times in my life when I wouldn't have even boarded that plane, never mind jumped out of it; times when all I wanted was a safe haven.

When we'd reached 8,000 feet, I'd asked the pilot to open the doors. At that moment, the butler had gone green and the comedian had turned white. I'd stuck my head out of the plane and felt the roar of the wind, beating against my face, which was already weathered by too many fights and a fair few life battles. The adrenalin surge in me was exhilarating. I knew deep down that something in me had changed forever. For long periods of my life, I didn't think I could handle whatever life had to throw at me, and I would often keep backing off, backing off... afraid to take the next step, the leap of faith that might separate my wildest dreams from a more muted reality.

Yet at that very second, I felt invincible.

What I did next changed my life.

I jumped.

# CONTENTS

# CHAPTER ONE
# TALLAGHTFORNIA

I always say that the second I was born, someone came down and sprinkled stardust on my head. Me ma Betty endured a 34-hour labour, much of it in an extremely distressed state. After all that pain, the midwife finally decided that she was unable to deliver me in the normal way and decided on an emergency Caesarean section. My da tells me it was extremely traumatic, not least due to the fact that when I finally came out, my head was stretched in a very alarming fashion, to the point at which he thought I was actually deformed. Da says he has never felt a shock like that when he first set eyes on me. He was only 21 at the time.

Fortunately, a nurse quickly reassured him that this was not uncommon and that my head would quickly form a normal shape, probably within a few hours. And thankfully, she was right. But that didn't stop me da praying and praying outside in the corridor when it all first happened. I was kept in an incubator for five days.

Looking at that moment, when I came into this world with a flat head, during a distressed birth, to where I have been and where I am right now, how could you doubt that stardust had indeed been sprinkled on me?

I was born in a hospital in Churchtown, central Dublin, and my family lived nearby in Kimmage. I don't remember a lot about our time there, as I was less than two when we left. I know that me da had a bakery there and that both him and mom worked incredibly hard. They were busy running this business and I wasn't a good sleeper. In fact, I was an awful sleeper, managing on only two or three hours a night. They used to have to take it in turns, shifts if you like, looking after me, because I seemed to need so little sleep. That's come in handy later in my life, let me tell you!

Back then, though, it was really hard work for them both and I admire them immensely for that. They'd met through work – Da's dad owned some supermarkets and me da used to drive a van picking staff up for work. Ma was one of those workers and she took a fancy to him. She chased him round and eventually they got together. She was 23 when they met, four years older than him. I've got me da's looks but me ma's personality – as a young woman, me ma was a proper party animal, the life and soul of the party. She still is, even to this day.

I have some pictures of me and my cousin sitting in this barrow contraption in me da's bakery, and Da is there with flour all over his face. I have no memory of that moment at all, to be honest – my first detailed memories all originate after Kimmage. Before that, it is mainly snapshots, flashbacks. Like when my little brother Gerry was born just after a six-month spell of the family living in Bray, County Wicklow. I would have only been two-and-a-half years old, but I can recall sitting in the car next to this tiny new baby, on our way back from the hospital. Da had a beard and was driving a boxy green Ford; I kept looking down at my new little brother for the whole journey. I also vaguely remember one Christmas, charging him around the sitting room in his pushchair, bashing into furniture and having a great time with him.

I am very close to both my brothers. That little baby Gerry has grown up to become a legend now, a proper tough man. We grew up together – not just in the same house, but *together*. Gerry always got away with murder because every time there was a problem it was always seen as my fault! In fact, he was usually the more crazy of us and I tended to be more reserved, but if we had a fight instead of keeping it quiet, Gerry would shout about it and I would end up getting told off. Me da would say, 'Fran! Leave your brother alone!' We had some great holidays as a family in the country and me and Gerry were inseparable at times. He is less than three years younger than me, so the age gap was a good one; the simple fact that we hung around together a lot, we were into the same things at the same time, like skateboarding, made us great mates. Gerry is wicked and we still get on really well.

Sometimes me da was a lunatic, though! When my second brother Adam was born, me ma was staying at me grandmother's to recuperate. I was staying with them too. Me da climbed up a lamppost and took me out of the bedroom window to go off with all his mates for the day. I can't quite remember the details but I have flashbacks of them all standing on the beach drinking a beer. And I wonder where I get me mad side from…!

Adam was a bit of a surprise – he is almost ten years younger than me. Growing up, that seemed to be a massive age difference, but he's a great kid. He's way more relaxed than me and was brilliant at school. In fact, he's just finished at college and flies through all his exams. He is big into sports as well, rugby and stuff, so what with that and being great at school, he is the total opposite of me! Back then we used to take him to play pool and look after him, making sure he had fun. I was very, very protective of him but because I eventually left home quite young, Adam spent a lot more time growing up with Gerry than he did with me. He is a wicked kid and whenever I go back I spend a lot of time with him.

My early childhood memories centre around the estate we lived on in Tallaght, near Dublin. We moved there in 1980. Tallaght was a suburb of Dublin, about five miles to the west of the city. Years ago it had been a small village with a real old-fashioned sense of community spirit, but in the 1960s people were moved from the more dishevelled parts of Dublin into very large housing estates, Tallaght being one such centre of relocation. The problem was, the concentrated population explosion caused massive unemployment, there were drugs all over the gaff and certain areas of Tallaght were... well, not very nice places to live at all.

Where we lived – Old Bawn – was actually one of the few all-right places in Tallaght. Ours wasn't a council estate – people owned their houses, which was unusual for that side of Dublin. Parts of the area were very rough, but Tallaght was OK, in fact some people used to call it 'Tallaghtfornia'. Brian McFadden from Westlife always slags me off for living there, calling me posh! The problem was, Tallaght had so much bad publicity that anyone who came from there suffered for its reputation.

It was not posh, let me assure you of that. However, the estate was quite clean – we lived in one of the many cul-de-sacs that curled like rabbit warrens around the roads. Looking out of my window across the road, there was a house on the opposite corner and, for some reason, I remember the man who lived there was a diver, and always had his diving gear out. The neighbour on the left side was a prick. My parents didn't get on with him – he was a weird old bastard, Polish I think. It's funny what things stick in your mind as a young child.

All the houses were separated only by a small gap, so you could jump over the fences from door to door easily. We used to bang on every door until we got caught.

The first time I got caught was also the very first time I was bitten by a dog. The family two doors down had an Alsatian. I knocked on their door, a chase ensued (that the dog won) and I got myself bitten on the leg. It scared the shit out of me. I went inside to show Ma and Da and they were like, 'You bloody idiot, sort your head out!' I was afraid of dogs for years after that – no wonder really.

We had pets, but I didn't have much luck with them. We had a rabbit, but me da found it dead in the back garden one day; we all suspected one of our neighbours, who was a bit mad. Let's just say there were certainly crazy people on that estate as well as normal people. Ma and Da were very vexed by that.

We also had a dog, a golden Labrador, a classic dog it was. I loved him – he was wicked. He used to freak out all the time, wrecking the gaff and causing mayhem, so much so that Ma had to keep him in the garage. The problem was that whenever he was put out of the house, he used to wail all night long. One day, me ma and da told me the dog had 'gone off to live in the fields with the farmer'. I thought nothing odd about that. Years later when I was about 18 and round me mate's house watching *Friends*, one of the characters said their dog had also gone off to live in the fields with the farmer. All me mates laughed and I said, 'Weird, we had a dog who went off to live with a farmer.' When they told me that was what people said when their dog was put down, I was gutted! I rang me ma and said,

'Ma, did we put the dog down?' I'd lived under that illusion for well over a decade!

Part of the patchwork of memories I have is playing 'nick nack', as we used to call it. You would go up to somebody's front door and ring the bell or knock as hard as possible and then run for your life. The game is called 'knock down Ginger' in England. It was best when we repeated it as many times as we could, causing maximum amount of distress to the people who lived in the houses, but also leading to the best chases.

I was a dootz when I was young, I tell you. There was this girl who lived down the road and I always fancied her, I really had a crush on her but couldn't get up the nerve to say something. Now, as kids we believed that if you gave someone you fancied a ring, they could make a wish; it was like a good luck charm. For weeks I was trying to muster up the courage to give a ring to this girl and finally I set off down the road on this big adventure, feeling smashing. I knocked on the door of her gaff and when her mom answered, I said in my most adult voice, 'Hello, how are you doing? I want to give this to your daughter.' I think the ring had cost half a pence from a toy shop! This woman was in shreds, trying not to laugh and still, to this day, I can remember her face. At the same time, although her little girl was only in primary school, you could see a part of her was thinking, *Oh my God, it's started...*

The whole extended family was close, all my cousins, and we often used to spend a lot of time together when we were younger. My parents used to hang around at my uncles' and aunts' houses – they all got on really well, especially my da and his brother Dave. My Uncle Jimmy was a former BMX champion, so I really got into that and rallying as a young kid. As I grew older I went to all the trials and races. It was great. I used to ride around the block all day, at the time it felt like I was going to Fiji, a real big man, but in a car the whole journey would only take about two minutes. I did quite well at BMX, but even back then I was scared of failing – a feeling that would stay with me for years to come – so I didn't do as well as I probably could have. Yet the contradiction was always in me that, despite this lack of confidence, I liked to challenge myself... to scare myself, even.

I was with my Uncle Jimmy the first time I watched Michael Jackson's *Thriller* video. We were sitting round his house with loads of people – he was popular when he was young. I was watching this werewolf mini-movie and I was terrified, screaming. Then me nanny came in and bollocked everyone because it had upset me – 'What are you doing? He's just a kid!'

Jimmy used to say, 'You're always dropping us in it.' He used to take me with him to go to visit birds' houses. I would get to these places and he'd be snogging these women in the car and I'd be like, 'What am I doing here?' We were walking home one night with this bird and I had to stand on a corner whistling while he kissed her goodnight! One time we went to this girl's house and on the way it was pouring down with rain. We got absolutely soaked through, so Jimmy stuck his trousers in the tumble-dryer and was sitting there in the lounge with just his pants on. Now, me nanny would not have approved of this, she was a beautiful lady but her generation was obviously more strict with certain things. So Jimmy said to me, 'When we get back to your nanny's, don't say a word, not a word!' We went home and I walked straight into me nan's sitting room and shouted, 'Uncle Jimmy had his trousers off and put them in the tumble-dryer!' There was murder! Jimmy was telling me 'You're a rat!' I was such a tell-tale at that age.

I always looked to my Uncle Jimmy for advice. One time I took him a copy of Bros's album and showed it to him. 'White socks are out, lad,' he told me. 'Never wear white socks, only black.' That's stuck with me all my life. At the time I was like, 'Woah!', as if I was getting some top-secret fashion advice.

It's funny how when you are that little, your immediate environment is your whole world. Back then, it was a huge, vast spread of enormous houses, kids on the big green playing, little burrows and lanes behind the houses leading to this world outside. All the roads were huge and it seemed like a massive journey to go anywhere. I've been to the estate in Tallaght several times as an adult and it just looks like a matchstick town. When I visit I can recall all the places and buildings from my childhood, but everything looks like it is in miniature compared to the way it is in my memories.

Walking past the diver's house, you came to a wall.

But not just any old wall: *the* wall. Over the top of that wall was 'No-Man's-Land', a patch of wasteland, scrub, bushes, some rubbish – somewhere kids shouldn't be playing, basically. All the kids' parents were constantly warning them about going over this wall. 'There's thousands of huge rats over there,' some of the kids used to say. That was enough to stop most children. My parents told me, 'If you see any rats, don't box them in. But most of all, DO NOT GO OVER THAT WALL!'

I wanted to know what it was like over the wall. No, not just 'wanted'... I *had* to know.

I used to sit on the top of it for ages, looking at the scrub, searching with my eyes, trying to spot these rats. Then I would go back in for tea or carry on playing. No one ever actually jumped over into No-Man's-Land. I was always terrified of that wall, but fascinated by it too.

*'Do not go over that wall.'*

I vividly remember the first time I did.

I was five or so, and we were all out in the street playing among ourselves. Every night at about 5pm there would be around fifty kids playing on the road. To me it felt like a very close-knit community. It was certainly a very different environment to today – I wouldn't let me kid Josh out of my sight now, I swear to God if he disappears out of my sight for a second I panic. But back then, the roads of the estate were our playground and we lived out there. This particular day, while everyone else was playing in the road, I started climbing up on top of the wall. There must have been something about the look in my eye that afternoon because gradually all the kids stopped playing and turned to watch me scale the wall. Next thing, I was standing on the top, one step from safety, one from being over the wall.

'Don't go over the wall, Fran!' one of me mates yelled.

I was scared.

But I jumped.

It was a bigger drop than I had imagined because on the house's side the pavement was built up, but I landed OK. I planted my feet on the ground and stood still for a moment. I remember thinking, *I am on dangerous ground.* If I were to go back and visit this scrubland today it would probably just look like a small field with a few plants in it, but at that precise moment, it felt like some massive expanse of treacherous wasteland. I turned back to the wall and to my horror realised I couldn't climb back up. The drop was just too big.

I was stranded over the wall.

'Holy shit! How am I gonna get back up?' I said out loud.

My heart was thumping out of my chest and I was scared. I knew that if I got caught me ma and da would be furious. I scurried around this scrubland for a while, then eventually realised that the only way to get back would be to walk all the way around the block, which was the longest journey *ever*. Later in life all sorts of situations would come my way: I've been shot at; people have lunged at me with knives more times than I care to remember; I've sped through a sniper's alley in the Middle East... But let me tell you, the thought of walking through that scrubland and all the way back home was one of the most terrifying I have ever faced. It was such a genuine feeling of fear, of the unknown.

It was only as I grew up from a Dublin boy into an Irish man that I realised it is the unknown that draws me in. It fascinates me.

CHAPTER TWO

# THE FIRST SIGNS OF DARKNESS

My first school was an old Christian boys' school in Tallaght called St Maelruans, where I went from the age of four until I was eight (at which point we moved to Dun Laoghaire). I'd already made my mark in kindergarten when I was caught snogging a girl one day and me ma was dragged in!

I was only eight when I left St Maelruans, so I have a limited memory of my time there. But I do remember being told I was going up to the big school. Da had been launching his new video shop at the time – he was the first person in Ireland to open a 24-hour video shop – so Ma took me up to St Maelruans for my very first day. I'd like to say I was the five-year-old hard man and walked in there no problem, but I have to admit I cried like a girl. I was desperate for me ma not to go and leave me. They took me into the classroom but I carried on bawling; in the end I cried so badly they had to sit me in the corner. I still remember to this day the emotion, being so upset and thinking, *This is all new, this is dangerous, I don't under-stand this; I don't like this.*

The school had a brutal brown uniform that I hated. I found my whole time in school quite difficult, to be frank with you. I've got a problem retaining information and this made classes quite a challenge. When I was very young I was given extra tuition, but it was always a struggle. To this day, if I try to read for too long, I get a headache, a strong pain in my head; it's weird. Of course, if you are not around the right sort of teacher, this difficulty can often be misinterpreted or – at best – not worked on.

We would occasionally go on a school trip. The first time we all went to the zoo with school, me ma gave me this Scotch egg. I went shopping to get 'supplies' for the trip with Ma and she picked it out for me – I thought I was dead grown-up with this egg, for some reason. I remember as soon as I got on the coach to go to the zoo, I ripped the wrapper off and gobbled up half of it in one mouthful – but it was disgusting so I spat it all out, 'Urrgghh!'

I had a phase of watching scary movies, I remember. When I was eight years old, I won an award in class. It was the first thing I'd ever won; it didn't mean much, but I won it. I wrote this story about Santa Claus. I thought to myself, *Claus? Claws!*, and made up this character with razor-sharp claws who came to your house on Christmas morning and chopped up your ma and da. The story was pretty weird and very dark, but to my amazement they actually decided it was the winner! Given that I was getting extra tuition and catching my fair share of disapproving frowns from unsympathetic teachers because I struggled in class, this was a huge triumph for me.

About nine weeks later, a teacher brought a book into school, one I had never heard of but which was similar to the story I had written. In front of the whole class, this teacher said, 'I knew you didn't write that, Cosgrave, you just copied it.' He'd made up his mind about me and was delighted he'd 'proved' himself right. I was gutted, even though I hadn't copied anything.

Undeterred, I tried to lever a bit of horror into the school's drama productions. The film *Shocker* is about a man who gets electrocuted, so I came up with the concept of trying to stage that movie at school – for eight-year-olds! I had an electric chair and a trap door and a big pulley, and it was all cunningly engineered so that these kids would fall into this hole with this mask on and get electrocuted.

Ma and Da got brought in about that.

In fact, they got brought in a few times.

We were a Catholic family, but I never felt comfortable with what that involved. To be honest, I hated it. Everyone went to Mass on Sundays – *everyone*. I just wasn't into it, but it was an integral part of all our lives. Me ma and da always went and so did me nanny, who took it very seriously. If we were at Nanny's, we would sometimes go to Mass twice each Sunday.

I dug out my Communion video a while back – I was only seven at the time. You would get all dressed up and there'd be a big party afterwards. You can see that I am saying these words but I haven't got a clue what I am talking about – 'It means that you get a Holy burn in your heart...' Even at that young age, I had a problem with authority. Basically, I thought that if you are going to say stuff, you should believe it, or at the very least understand it. In the years since we all went to Mass, things have changed a lot, and for many people in Ireland there has been a massive shift in the reality of the Church. But back then it was, 'This is what you believe in, this is how you follow that, this is what you do and this is what you don't do.'

Mind you, there were some fringe benefits of going to Mass – me nanny used to spoil us rotten, for one. I always used to have chip sandwiches with ketchup, which I loved. Ah, God – I can still taste them as I write! And if Uncle Jimmy was there we would make an assault course in the garden, dragging mattresses out there to climb over and setting up high jumps with sticks and all that. We had such a great time, but when we went home Ma had to rein us back in pretty quickly. 'It's not like your nanny's here, you know!' she used to say; it drove her mad. I used to always love it when we went to me Nanny's.

One great thing about the Catholic way, however, was that each milestone – whether it be a Communion, Confirmation or whatever – provided a great excuse for a party; a respectful reason for everyone to go on the piss. I used to love those parties, my parents' gaff was always buzzing, people were coming around, having a great time. Funnily enough, one pub in Rathfarnham where we often celebrated became my main local when I was a teenager.

These social occasions were also the first real time that boys started to see girls other than at school. I fancied girls even when I was really young – I think I had my first kiss when I was only about four. We all used to go and see this singer on a Sunday – Paul Duffy was his name, and his whole family was performers – at this pub called The Foxhunter. I always used to fancy Maria, Paul's little sister. But I was too shy to mention anything back then. I was madly in love with her but never said a word.

I loved our house – it was such an exciting place to grow up, there was always a party going on. I remember people pouring through the house most nights. I have such fond memories of those parties; everyone seemed so happy. I can remember being about four or five and sitting on me dad's lap while they were supping beer and having a great time. Trivial Pursuit was a big obsession at one point; people were really into that and playing other board games as well. I used to sit and listen to the questions even though I didn't know any answers at that age. I used to look at me ma and da and they were such good parents. They have had some mad times but they are still together after nearly thirty years. That's good going!

As I grew older, we continued to have some wild times in the house, full-on lunatic parties. If it wasn't at our house, we'd often go out to one somewhere else. Me and me parents were driving back from a party one night with a bloke who insisted he was a dog – so they put him in the boot. We got stopped by the cops, who only realised he was in there because he was barking so loudly. I was only a kid and was really worried about what the police would say. But this officer lifted the boot up, took one look at this barking man and then put it straight back down, advising us to get him home before he bit someone!

In 1985, when I was seven, we left Tallaght and went to live in Dun Laoghaire. I was sent to St John's School in Ballybrack. Obviously, being the new boy was difficult for me. The problem was that at St Maelruans I had known everyone and had my little circle of friends, plus I knew the school and was comfortable in my surroundings. Moving to a new school is never easy and so it proved for me in St John's. I started to become withdrawn. I wasn't a big lad, so I wasn't particularly capable of looking after myself either and I began to get bullied.

It was brutal for a few years, a very dark phase when I got picked on mercilessly for some time, and I ended up withdrawing from life almost completely for the best part of a year. I wasn't particularly small, but I was 'the new kid' and that cost me. I hated school and I hated life. To make matters worse, I still wasn't good in class, and they kept me back – I was always seen as 'a kid who is not going to make it'. This didn't help me integrate in the playground either.

The truth of the matter was that I was dyslexic and that's why I hadn't been progressing and keeping up with the rest of the kids. Dad used to sit with me to help with my homework and it would take *forever*. It used to drive him mad – it took ages – but he never stopped helping me, fair play to him. Every night he would sit down with me at the table for hours, and all this after God-knows how many hours at work.

He used to take me and five or six of my mates into Dublin to a park, where he would run around for three hours playing soldiers. Me da was my best friend and he was my mates' best friend too. Even though I was only young, I noticed how loads of other dads were off taking the piss, drinking, going with other women, but my da was nothing like that. When I think of how busy him and Ma were yet they still found time for us like they did, it's incredible. To think of me running around with my son Josh and six of his mates in a park for hours on end... I've got to be perfectly honest with you: I can't see it. But me da used to do that all the time.

Unfortunately, school life was still pretty tough. There were a few times when I had the shit kicked out of me. The trouble was, I just wasn't strong enough to do anything about it. Me ma and da weren't aware of it either.

In truth, I think I am one of the luckiest people in the world. Why? Because I've been on the receiving end of this stuff but I haven't come away all bitter and twisted. You know what? Even though I couldn't fight back – at that point in my life, anyway – I did feel a sense of perspective about this sort of intimidation. 'I am gonna make it better, make people feel happy rather than make people feel bad.' I love to see people happy. Being bullied made me realise that.

At primary school, I always felt out of the main group and, naturally, I wanted to be part of the in-crowd – as you do at that age. Years later, when people were telling me I was cool and knew all the right faces in London and all that, the compliments meant nothing to me – by then, I had grown up and had more perspective. But as a lad, I wasn't part of the cool crowd at all, and it made me very sad. The bullying was almost a definitive way of telling me I was an outsider.

When people see me jumping into a pool full of crocodiles or jumping out of a plane or standing with twenty doorman who follow every word I say, it gives a certain impression. Go back to those early school years and it wasn't like that at all. But that's one of the contradictions about me. Outside I have always had that outward confidence, but for long periods of my life I have really lacked inner self-belief and strength – certainly compared to what a lot of people might expect.

I was a scared kid for a long time.

# CHAPTER THREE

# WHAT ME DA TOLD ME WHEN I WAS YOUNG

When I was twelve, we were sent up to the secondary school – The Presentation College in Glasthule, Dun Laoghaire. That is where so many things changed in my life – where I got bullied, where I learned to stand up for myself, where I started seeing girls, going to clubs, having a fair few scraps... it was a pivotal few years in my life.

I hated the uniform. I used to try to subvert it any way I could, so I'd wear trainers even though you were supposed to wear black shoes. You had to wear black trousers too, but I went and bought some huge, over-sized black suit trousers so they couldn't really argue but at least I looked a little cool. I bought a top too that was similar to the regulation uniform, but again a little bit more cool, just so I didn't have to wear the school jumper.

At The Presentation College, myself and quite a few of me mates constantly tried to bend what rules there were by growing our hair long, even though the school didn't allow it. After a face-off, a compromise was reached and we all had to tie our hair up, but eventually the authorities won the day and I cut it off.

When I went to the first year of secondary, I was quite a lot bigger than everyone else because of being kept back a year, due to my difficulties in class. I knew I found the work harder than most of my mates so I did what I have done all my life and found a way around the obstacle. In this instance, I learned how to master the art of distraction. I used to be able to distract a situation so completely I would end up in control of it and therefore not have to engage with stuff I found difficult. Sometimes I would distract the teachers so comprehensively that no one else in class got any work done either.

Don't get me wrong, I did like some aspects of school. I have a massive love for history and I quite liked geography – the only teacher I ever respected in my life was our geography teacher Mr Flynn. And do you know why I liked him? Because he was a normal bloke, who spoke to every kid with respect as if they were a normal person too whereas everyone else just spoke to us as an authority figure. When you were in his class, people would actually listen, whereas with most of the other teachers no one would pay any attention. Those teachers would just scream, 'Get an education!' That's a big reason why me and school didn't always combine too well – I'm not big on authority, it's just something that doesn't fit in with my life. Every time they ever said 'no' to me at school, I used think, *I'm going to find a way around you.* I still do to this day.

I learnt to survive on my wits rather than my academic ability. This meant that I started to learn skills other than the ABCs of the classroom, such as reading body language, judging someone's mood, observing a situation and deciding in an instant how to get the best results out of it. I learnt to look at people and read them. I knew what pushed people's buttons and what didn't. That led me to understand people more, which in turn came in very handy later in life, when I started working doors.

Also, I was a good talker. As a kid, I often thought I was stupid, especially with the problems I had in class, but at the same time I knew I was really switched on to life's experiences. In secondary school, the Irish teachers would have debates about certain things and I would love to challenge them. I was able to hold a very serious conversation with them, too. A few of the teachers liked me because I was bit more grown-up, and looking back, I guess I was acting more like an adult most of the time. So I did get an education from school after all – though not the conventional one.

All the teachers thought I was a lunatic at secondary and they wanted me to go and see a counsellor to talk about stuff; they said I had 'pent-up anger'. So I went to see this bloke, sitting in his chair all prim and proper, black curly hair with a round, slightly chubby face that didn't really match his body. He had a tweed jumper on with corduroy trousers and his legs crossed, anchored by a pair of the sort of shoes that headmasters wear, which he clearly polished every morning, I am sure. I sat down on this couch and he said to me, 'So tell me about yourself' and I thought to myself, *I am going to mess with your head.*

He asked me to draw a picture so I sketched this image of a burning house, all these people screaming and running, someone else holding a knife and he was like, 'Oh my God!' He said there was so much anger in this picture, but I just did it to wind him up. I asked him what we were going to do and he said talk.

'But if I don't talk, you don't talk?'

'People usually start off these sessions like that, Fran.'

So I sat there for an hour in silence. It was the longest hour of my life. Then when the clock got to the hour, I said, 'That's time, isn't it?' and he said, 'Yes,' so I left. Me da was waiting outside for me and he asked how I got on and I said, 'Oh, it was brilliant, he's really good.' (My da is going to kill me when he reads this!)

I went to see this counsellor for about nine months, but I barely spoke to him. I used to go in, shake his hand and sit down in silence. After a few weeks he said, 'Don't you think you've proved your point, Fran?' and I did speak a little more later but not much. I think it frustrated him that he couldn't get through to me and it ended up being quite personal. Actually, I feel bad thinking about that now – I made his life a misery. Still, I was just a kid.

I wasn't really ever into the usual sports kids love, like football, but when I was very young, around five, me da had started taking me to karate lessons. I used to go two or three times a week for years – one of the karate clubs we used was this freezing, dirty old hall where you would always get splinters in your feet. Da was not especially the sporty type, but he used to come along as well. I think part of the attraction for me was that at that young age I wanted to be what any self-respecting kid did when he grew up: a Ninja.

As I grew up I kept going and got pretty good at it, though I struggled with the techniques, the discipline, the authority side of that martial art – I wasn't really into it that much, I just really liked fighting. By the time I was about 13, I was entering competitions and fighting against 40-year-old men... and winning. Although I was a tall kid, I was also pretty slim but that didn't stop me triumphing, sometimes even against black belts. My own belts slipped back quite often because I didn't enjoy the exams and the technical expectations. There was something you needed to keep applying yourself to, but I didn't: I just fought. It was about protecting myself against the bullies at school and it wasn't about being hard or rough; I just wanted to be a Ninja. I didn't need to prove anything to anyone else, especially not by taking an exam. I'm not the exam type.

By my early teens, I was giving karate classes to all the local kids – in my parents' garage! I would come home from my own karate lesson in the evening, and the day after would teach my mates the blocks and stuff I had learnt the previous day. I guess you could say that was pretty disciplined, to be fair. Strangely enough, although being good at karate was without doubt an asset, I don't ever recall thinking – consciously, at least – that it gave me more confidence.

I was still getting my fair share of grief at school, but I was gradually learning to stand up for myself. Good martial-arts classes will always advise against using the skills you learn on the street unless absolutely necessary, so I recall vividly the very first time I put my knowledge of karate to use during a fight at school. A few kids had been pushing me around, bullying me and generally making my life a misery. One day they started trying to beat me up and I was terrified, but I scrapped and I did it quite well. Eventually, I had had enough and when this one kid came for me again, I did this thing where I ducked around, got him in a headlock and came down on his back – he collapsed on the spot and everyone stopped dead in their tracks.

He was on the ground and he wasn't getting up.

I remember looking at him and thinking, *Fuck! What have I done to this person?* I got off home and sat down, still wondering what I had done to him. At the time he was the coolest kid in the school as well, good-looking and liked by everyone, which somehow made the impact of it all greater. I didn't tell me ma and da, partly because I couldn't believe I'd done that to somebody. I actually felt remorse. I have never taken glee from fighting or scrapping, I'd never take pride or get a buzz from anything like that, unlike a lot of people I know. It turned out he was fine and because no one said anything to the teachers, I didn't get in any trouble about it. Mind you, they didn't pick on me again either.

Over time, as it became apparent I could look after myself the bullying subsided until it pretty much stopped altogether. In fact, by the time I was about 14, I had started to work out using a few basic weights in me da's garage and what with me getting a little bigger and my reputation for doing karate, I was no longer the whipping boy.

However, my own experiences of being bullied made me feel almost duty-bound to be some kind of Robin Hood figure. I knew the kids who would always get bullied and picked on and I did my best to step in and look after them. I don't mean that to sound corny, but it wasn't right and this time I was big enough and strong enough to do something about it. My brothers had an easy ride through school because all the bad lads left them alone!

It was through this impulse for looking out for weaker kids that I met one of my future best (and ex-best) mates, Nick. I was only a first year and he was in the fifth and final year, so there was quite an age gap. How we met was classic. When we used to come in from break time, you had to walk past all the years in order along this corridor. It really was like running the gauntlet because as you did, older boys used to drag the younger kids into empty classrooms and beat the shit out of them.

One afternoon this particular little kid was taking a real beating; they were killing him. I couldn't stand up for every single kid getting hit but this was way too harsh, so I ran in the room and smacked the biggest kid – who turned out to be Nick – and he proceeded to chase me down the corridor. He quickly caught hold of me and we started fighting right there and then, in the corridor, in front of the whole school. He got me in a headlock so I went down on my knee, then punched my head upwards and bashed him in the face, knocking him to the ground. A teacher came running over and grabbed me but in the heat of the scrap, I elbowed him in the face. That was the first time I met Mr McNally! He was a very strict German teacher, so I hadn't chosen well. Still, it was better than hitting 'Brick' – Mr Walsh – an English teacher. He was called Brick because he was dead stern and you wouldn't mess with him, but always very cool, a good teacher. Needless to say, I got a hefty detention, but everyone thought I was great – when we were fighting they were shouting, 'Go on, Fran!'

I also met a friend I have to this day – Barry – through scrapping. Both he and Nick came from Rathfarnham, and I quickly started to meet up with their crowd. It was mad where we hung around up there in Pine Valley. All the kids were mentallers, seriously! Everyone was drinking, smoking, shagging each other – it was one of those estates... I don't know how we got away with it, I really don't.

We used to have this young disco at the Wesley where we would get steaming drunk and meet loads of people. Every Friday we would get dressed up in new clothes, meet up with the lads, get some drink to get us buzzing and head off to the disco. The shit going on was unbelievable – dozens of people kissing on the rugby field... wild times. I used to get off with ten or fifteen girls a night! It was chaos! It's funny because looking back I met most of my Dublin friends as a result of having that first fight with Nick.

I'll be honest, though: Nick was not a good friend in the end. At the time, I was working part-time for my dad at his video shop and always had money in my pocket and new clothes to wear. I'd bought myself a beautiful pair of Air Jordans. Nick borrowed them one afternoon but the next day he came in and said, 'I got beaten up on the bus and they took your runners off me.' Then about two weeks later we were hanging around one of the estates and a mate of mine came down wearing my shoes!

Looking back, some pretty mad stuff went on at my school. Pupils attacked teachers, which was bad enough, but some teachers even attacked pupils! One time this teacher had smashed a chair over this kid, so I dived in and pulled him off. Another time, I was sitting next to this kid when the teacher started slagging off his parents, saying they were 'alcoholic bastards'. Understandably the kid freaked out and went up to fight the teacher, so I ended up holding them apart while some other teacher was called in. I loved wading in and sorting things out. I am not a violent or a hard person, but I felt like I had to do something for everybody who couldn't do it for themselves. If I saw it going on I *had* to do something about it. I actually took pride in that.

Often, I would end up dishing out advice to some of these kids. It makes me laugh to think of it now, but I used to make up all sorts of phrases and sayings to explain the point I was trying to make. I knew people wouldn't necessarily listen to all this coming from just a kid, so I used to preface it by saying, 'Me da told me...' For example, I told one mate: 'Me da told me, it's not how bad you fall off the horse, it's how well you get back on that people will remember.' I used to come out with them all the time, unbeknown to me da, but one day I did the decent thing and phoned him up, told him and said, 'Da, you must be the wisest man in the world!'

Of course, I still got in occasional fights myself. I was almost always in control, but I had this fear inside about what would happen if I completely lost it. To an extent I still do today, because I'm scared that if I ever let go too much I could get in a lot of trouble. You should never lose control in a fight situation.

I can remember the first time that it happened to me at school. These two blokes had been picking on me for ages and for the first time ever, I just lost it and they got a right beating. I got kicked out of school for about three weeks after that. It was one of the only times in my life that I lost my grasp on reality for a few seconds, I was just gone. That was a scary experience and not one I want to repeat. In my defence it was brought on by being pushed and pushed, and poked and poked to the point where I fucking exploded. But the most frightening aspect of it all was knowing I'd been out of control.

I don't want to make my school sound like it was scrapping all day, every day, though. We had some great times. Break times were dead boring, so I got them to put a basketball court in the yard and all the hard lads started playing these games every day. We all got pretty good and these matches became more and more intense. It was like a scene out of *The Shawshank Redemption*, those fierce prison-yard contests. It got to the point where my school day revolved around break times, half an hour in the morning, an hour for lunch and half an hour in the afternoon to play basketball.

I spent half the day in the toilet smoking. You could go down there between classes and we'd all be doing the same thing, puffing away in the toilets. It was always the same people sneaking out, a little social club in the loos. I can't believe we used to do that and get away with it.

Naturally, girls were a major factor of school life for me too. But I was a bit of a dootz, and was never really good at talking to them. I just didn't have the confidence to talk to them – even now, if I was single, I would struggle to chat one up. I didn't have the confidence to do a lot of things – probably a consequence of feeling scared a lot as a kid, I suppose.

Music began to take over my life during secondary school. I started listening to a very weird mix of sounds. The first time I heard Cypress Hill was in a film called *Juice*, where they were playing at a house party. I loved that film. Before that I had seen one of Tupac's films and loved the tunes on that as well. I wanted to buy every record that NWA and Ice-T had ever made too. At the same time, I was heavily into the Pixies, Dead Kennedys and Ned's Atomic Dustbin. I used to listen to Ned's when I was doing my homework. In the same evening I would mix up rap with James Taylor and Cat Stevens, then more Ned's, then *Straight Outta Compton*. A lot of my mates were really into The Doors and although I can see Jim Morrison's star appeal, I could write better poetry than that pissed, let's be honest...

I always dressed different from all the other kids. I wanted to have something unique and my own. I was a little bit weird, I'll admit that, but at least I was trying to make a statement. I had a phase of wearing Doc Martens and grandfather shirts then I was heavily into skateboarding and all that gear. Always looking for something different. When I started to dress in a certain way, people gave me stick, saying I was trying to be a black man. They called me 'Fran X' at one point. But I didn't care: I simply loved listening to all sorts. That's how my mind was opened up to experiences I had later – raving, DJ-ing and eventually clubland.

By now I was hanging out with Nick and his mates a lot, lads who were much older than me, so perhaps inevitably I started getting insights into things that were beyond my years. I was only young, but I grew up far quicker than I should have. I wouldn't want my own son, Josh, to be as far ahead of his classmates – in certain things – as I was.

One time my parents were away and I was being 'baby-sat' by a girl who worked in me da's video shop. We bunked off school and went into Dublin on the back of a bus. On the way, the bus lurched in the traffic and as it did, my rucksack fell open and a bottle of vodka tumbled out, then proceeded to roll down the centre aisle of the bus in front of every passenger, almost as if it was happening in slow motion. It came to rest against the very front seat. Now I had the dilemma of what to do. I didn't want to waste a whole bottle of vodka by leaving it there, but picking it up was a shameless admission it was mine. I picked it up.

We made it back home, but my problems had only just begun. Me da was one step ahead of us, because he'd arranged for one of his mates to call round at our house that night to check up on us. By this time, a few of the lads had had too much to drink so when there was a knock at the door and me da's mate was standing there, a couple of them panicked. One of them was upstairs and when he heard me da's mate's voice, he jumped out of a bedroom window, slid down a drainpipe, legged it down the garden and leaped over our fence into the field at the back, which was full of horses. Other mates were hiding in cupboards and clothes presses – it was hilarious.

To be honest, I didn't bunk off that often, simply because it got you in too much trouble. At lunchtime we weren't even allowed out of the school grounds, but we used to slide out through the fence every day for an hour regardless. Wednesday was a half-day so we would pile into town and play pool all day at this pub called The Hideout. You had to press the doorbell to get in and they would look out through this little spy-hole to see who it was – you can imagine, to a teenage boy this was deadly. Everyone hung around in The Hideout; we used to virtually live in the place.

The first time I got caught drunk was in The Hideout. One afternoon we were coming out of there when this policeman grabbed me and my bags.

'What's all this?' he asked, like he'd just apprehended some international criminal.

I had some new clothes in my bag.

'You tell me you robbed these clothes and I will let you go.'

'Do I look like an idiot, mate?'

'I am going to ring your parents,' he countered.

'Bollocks! Do you have to?'

'Well, you go straight home and tell them what you've been up to. I'll call them in an hour to check, OK? Now, go home and tell them.'

I didn't go home. I got on a bus and went to a mate's to

get even drunker. I had started to worry, though, and I was like, 'You don't think he is actually going to phone my ma, do you?' The next thing I knew these lads came running in – laughing, to be fair – saying, 'Your ma is ringing round looking everywhere for you!' The police had kept to their word and told her. Then I heard her car out in the street and she came and dragged me back home in front of all me mates. I was fucking mortified; it was one of the most embarrassing moments ever. She was furious, she wasn't speaking – she got in the car and just growled at me. We drove home in silence and me da was like, 'What were you thinking?' Let's face it, at that age, you get good at hiding things. It wasn't the first time I had got drunk, but it was just the first time I had got caught.

I was grounded for eight weeks, me ma would not let me out of the gaff. At that age, it felt like an eternity, I was so bored out of my mind. Eventually, I got myself these crap belt-driven turntables – for £102 – and taught myself to DJ in that two-month window, working on breakbeat tunes and jungle. Listening to that music made me happy. One of my mates went and got a load of breakbeat and happy hardcore tunes to work on – which was very English, no one in Ireland really liked it. (I always thought I should have lived in England, just from the music point of view, the music I was into was always from there – all the big, happy hardcore raves and all that.) I didn't really have my own record collection until much, much later. At this point I didn't know anyone who DJ-ed, so no one was able to teach me how to do it.

From the earliest age all I ever wanted to do was music. When I was five I would sit writing songs and singing them in my garage, but as I grew older I never had enough confidence to do anything with it. For a while I wanted to learn saxophone, but they started you off with a recorder – the only trouble with me was that I wouldn't do any practice, so that didn't go any further. Mind you, to be fair, Paul Oakenfold was never going to make millions from being a professional superstar recorder player.

When I was a teenage kid, I wanted to be a musician (apart from a brief phase of wanting to be a vampire and, of course, a Ninja). Apart from family, the most joy I have got out of life is from listening to music. It makes my brain tick. Although I would have loved to be in one, I didn't have the confidence to be in a band, but I did feel good enough about myself to start DJ-ing.

At that point I wasn't really interested in putting on parties. I didn't follow any superstar DJs as such, I wasn't into the celebrity of it, I just liked working the decks – though the late Tony De Vit was someone I aspired to, because he had such energy. I'd look at DJs and think, *This is what I want to do: I want to stand in front of people and make them dance.* I will never forget how shit I was on the decks, though... Oh my God, I was awful at first! People used to let me have a go at playing at parties, 'Go on give him a shot', but in the space of two records I could empty a room. I remember we went to one party where they had a set of the mythical 12-10s set up, the Holy Grail of decks at that point. I stood and stared at them for ages, then when someone said I could have a session I nearly fell over in the rush to get behind them. I sauntered up there – for all the world a superstar DJ in the making. For a few minutes I looked around trying to be cool. But eventually I had to say something:

'Er, excuse me, how do you turn this thing on?'

# CHAPTER FOUR

# SPIRALLING WITH THE TRIBES

By the end of secondary school, I had started to live the life of a young adult – clubbing, drinking late and generally partying all the time. I always felt like I had an old head on my shoulders, and sometimes when I sat in class in my mid-teens, I felt out of place. I remember one Monday morning the kid sitting next to me said, 'I was playing football with my Dad all weekend,' and I was like, 'Mate, I was in the Mansion House raving until 5am!'

By the time I was 16 I had a 17-year-old girlfriend who drove a Mercedes. You can imagine at that age – when it is so important to have a nice-looking girlfriend – the shock on my mates' faces when she came to pick me up at the school gates in her Merc! 'See you later, lads!'

I still spent loads of time with Da. When playing at soldiers in the park had changed to going out clubbing, all the other dads had decided they couldn't give a shit, but my da used to come and pick us up from a club, drop all my mates off safely and then take me home. They used to call him Cosgrave Taxis. The best thing is, when he used to pick us up, we'd jump in the car and he'd be playing NWA's *Straight Outta Compton*. We'd all be banging along to this and I would be sitting in the back smiling, going, 'My Dad! My Dad!' In all fairness, the shit me dad has done all his life, he never stops. I often say to him, 'Sit down Dad, you've done your thing, relax!' I tell you, if I can only be a patch on what he was to me, I will be a happy person when I am taking my last vows, I swear to God.

Despite my general lack of interest in academic matters and my continued struggles with retaining information, I did actually sit the exams and managed to get six honours in the Junior Certificate. I was never going to go into further education, but I am actually pretty proud of what I achieved, given all the circumstances.

But I have to be honest: the way I looked at school was the same way I looked at Fiji or the jungle all those years later when I was a nightclub owner in London. Once I was there I had to be there, I had no choice and as soon as I had a choice, I left. I simply had to get through it. School did nothing for me. If I had stayed at school, maybe I could have got a better education, but I didn't and I've done OK. However – for any kids looking to me as an example – yeah, I left school at 15, but it's not the way to go. I broke my parents' rules, I broke my friends' rules, I broke the school rules... I would never advise a kid to drop out of school. It's just not a good idea. Stay in school.

I first went raving in 1991. It was New Year's Eve, the day after my birthday, so the timing was perfect. My dad dropped me off at the club called Raindance for the night. It was a massive deal for me. Ecstasy was starting to appear, though you couldn't get it at the club, but most people didn't know anything about the drug or the scene. At first, I didn't quite know what was going on. I walked into this gaff and liked it straight away. Initially I thought everyone was gay, though, because all the blokes were hugging each other. I thought, *This is a bit weird!* Then a few guys came up to me and I was like, 'Oi! Don't touch me!' However, within about twenty minutes I was really into the music and after about an hour I just thought, *Oh my God, what is this all about? It's brilliant!* By the end of the night, I was saying to myself, *This is what I want to do with my life.* It had that much impact; it changed everything for me. Of course, my Da being the fucking legend that he is, he picked me up at 3am the next morning.

From that moment on, the rave scene dominated everything I did. At that point, the entire phenomenon was totally underground. But that, of course, only added to the appeal – this whole mad world that no one's parents knew anything about. The atmosphere was so different to what I had been used to. There was definitely a mellower vibe about the rave community and you rarely, if ever, saw fights or heard of people being robbed – any petty crime was nearly always caused by people coming in from outside the scene. Of course, the ecstasy fuelled the happy atmosphere, partly because it meant people could dance for hours on end.

I had so many classic nights raving. I saw Spiral Tribe at the Hellfire Club up in Dublin, these old burnt-down buildings that were supposed to be haunted by the Devil. It was the most amazing outdoor party, absolutely mental. All these travellers had been going round doing these free parties. For obvious reasons, no one knew where the party was actually going to be, but a few phone calls would be made and people would head off to the rave. On this particular night, the party was up the mountains. I was going by myself so I got a taxi some of the way, but then got out to walk the rest of the journey. The only cars on this dark road were filled with people going to the rave. A car stopped and offered me a lift, so I hopped in – I wasn't thinking about whose car it was, whether it was safe to get in, I just knew we were all going to the same party. It was one of the best nights I have ever had. I remember sitting at five in the morning looking around this old burnt-out house full of ravers and thinking, *This is incredible!*

Inevitably, all that 'dancing' could catch up with you. After the Spiral Tribe show I was in a jock for about two days afterwards, covered in mud and dirt. This was what I lived for at weekends – I actually didn't socialise that much in the week because all my mates lived on the other side of town in Rathfarnham. But come Friday night, I was raring to go, a proper weekend lunatic. I loved it with a passion. Every Friday I would be off to the

Pine Valley and I wouldn't come back until Sunday. I wasn't robbing people or beating them up, I was just getting a pure buzz out of raving.

Those first few times I went, none of my usual mates were into it. From being a bullied kid at primary who wanted to go with the crowd most days, I'd grown up into my teens to be really quite single-minded. Even when I wasn't sure who I was or what I wanted from life, I was still ploughing my own furrow – loads of my mates were into The Doors and so were their girls, but I just didn't like that kind of stuff. To this day, if I want to go 'this way', that's where I will go. It was the same back then with raving. My mates were all very sceptical of it, warning me that I looked a state, but I said to them, 'I am telling you, you'll all be doing this soon, coming to these parties.' Then my mate Jerry decided to give it a go and his instant reaction was, 'This is deadly!' He was hooked that first night, just as I had been.

I liked the women as well – I met some great birds out raving. It wasn't really about that at the time to be honest, though, it was just about the 'dancing'. It was the first real release I'd ever got, just being able to close my eyes, stand there by myself dancing, no matter who I was or wasn't with. As I said, I often went to parties by myself, and loads of my mates thought I was a nutter.

Then slowly but surely raving started creeping into everyone else's life too. I started to see the tell-tale signs in other friends. There was a time when you were able to tell if people went to raves just by looking at them; you had a connection with them. They were hooked for the same reasons I was. It was something new and something different, not everyone was doing it, you met new people and experienced something totally different to your average Saturday night getting pissed and fighting all the time. You generally had an amazing time – it wasn't about being hard, everyone was just partying. It was completely cool.

In terms of commercial success, the biggest band on the scene was The Prodigy. The first time I went to see that band was in mid-1991. They were amazing. I went to this place called McGonagles, a famous venue where all the big-name bands played. Mad, it was. I was wearing my green trousers and red boots, a total raver.

Before we went into the gig, we grabbed a double vodka each and sat down drinking that, knocking it back as quick as we could – what were we doing, with all that dancing to come? I'd been with my dad to see bands he was into, Huey Lewis and the News, Belinda Carlisle and that kind of stuff, but I never really quite 'got' concerts. Even to this day, they bore me a little. Shows like that are too distant, too removed from the crowd. To get a buzz out of something, I am one of those people who has to be involved. When I was at clubs watching DJs, it spurred me on to practise more and more so that I could be like them; at raves, I felt like I was totally immersed in the middle of it all, even if I was on my own. It was absolute, total involvement. The weirdest thing is that fourteen years later the main man in The Prodigy – Liam Howlett

– helped put me in touch with Martin, my co-writer on this book. If you had told me, as a kid standing at the back of that Prodigy gig back in 1991, that I would even meet Liam, let alone write a book about my life, I would have not believed it possible.

While I was out raving one night, I saw this guy with his hair dyed white. I couldn't believe my eyes, I'd never seen anything like it before and it looked stunning. My ma used to use this really cool hairdresser called Dan and he came in Da's video shop all the time. He used to cut my hair in exchange for a free film. He was a bit of a cool bastard, and seemed to know the score about life. I used to talk to him about a lot of things and although he was an older guy he was a right mentaller. I always used to listen to him.

I remember getting my hair cut and telling him about these parties and it turned out that he knew a lot of the people already. I was very impressed! So I asked him to dye my hair white too. Nobody in Ireland had really seen this look before, apart from the ravers, so I knew it would get attention. After he'd done it for me, I walked out of the hairdresser's with this bleached-white hair and people on the street were stopping in their tracks to stare. I got down to the video shop and my dad was horrified: 'Jesus, Fran! What have you done? You can't work here with hair like that!'

I wasn't bothered about what the video-shop customers might think; I just couldn't wait until the weekend to get to a party. When I walked in everyone said it was wicked! Some of my mates still say to me I was ahead of my time – 'Remember that time you dyed your hair white, Fran?' I loved the fact that people would look at me and react. It's not that I liked the attention, I simply liked being different.

Eventually, of course, the rave scene started to lose its appeal for me, as it did for millions of others like me. All the 'dancing' had taken its toll on my health. I went from a healthy 14 stone to about 11 stone in a couple of months. One morning I woke up and went, 'Nah, I'm not feeling this any more.' I loved going to the parties but I just wasn't enjoying the physical side as much. Plus, my brain had started getting mashed – I was thinking about things too much and getting really fucked up. So the raving petered out or, at least, the 'dancing' did. I still carried on clubbing, though, that would never change.

In fact, by this point, I was a seasoned party animal, a total mentaller. I wanted to go to every club I could find, just to experience it and to party. There was this gay club in Dublin called Shaft that was so cool and I was desperate to go, but you couldn't get in unless you were gay. A load of us lads had tried and tried but the doormen were having none of it. I was desperate so one night myself and me mate walked up holding hands trying to look lovey-dovey, and the doorman was like, 'Lads! Come on!' Then he seemed to think about it a bit, and said, 'We know you are not gay but you deserve to get in and have a look.' So he let us in – and it was one of the best nights I've ever had!

My mate Jerry was one of my main partners in crime. Whenever we'd had a really late-night/early-morning session, we would always stay in his gaff – for two reasons. Firstly, his parents often had a few beers and would usually be asleep when we crawled in late. Secondly, his was a family of eight so the next morning, when you slid downstairs in a jock, no one really noticed because there were so many people moping around in the house. In contrast, whenever we stayed at my house, the next morning, me ma would come down, take one look at us and say, 'What the bloody hell is wrong with you?' Jerry's dad used to leave a mattress out on the floor and I would always race to get to sleep before Jerry because he was one of the loudest snorers in the world, and his dad was too. It seemed to be alternating in synch too, so it was like Dolby Surround Sound. Snoring, both ears getting it in exact unison. I still get on really well with Jerry and his parents; they're all lovely people.

Looking back, it's funny which events and situations turn out to be key moments in your life, even though at the time they are simply daily occurrences. Around this time, I went out on the town with my friend Jerry and the weirdest thing happened, something that was a crucial factor in my getting involved with clubs professionally. We were on our way into town, but couldn't find a taxi anywhere. Resigned to missing out, we started to head back to the housing estate, when out of nowhere this black Mercedes limousine pulled up, the driver wound his window down and asked us if we

needed a lift anywhere. We couldn't believe our luck –
limousines were not something you expected to see in
the estate, especially just when you needed a cab, but this
guy really was just a cabbie with a posh ride.

We sat in the back of the Merc having a chat with the
driver and we got on really well, he seemed like a really
nice bloke, sound. He told us that V Nasty was playing at
this club he knew of, and Nasty was proper big at the
time, so we were well up for that. The problem was, we
didn't exactly have a great track record for getting into a
lot of these clubs. But the cab driver said, 'Don't worry,
lads! I know all the doormen, you'll be fine.'

We got to this club and this cabbie just walked us
straight past this long, snaking queue and up to the front
door. He obviously did know the doormen because we
waltzed right in, then he took us to the bar and we were
handed free drinks. We couldn't actually believe it was
happening, neither of us had been treated like this
before, we felt like VIPs. They really looked after us; it was
easily one of the best nights I've ever had. The next day,
we were chatting about it and reliving every moment
and I thought to myself, *I want to be able to do that all the
time.* I don't know why, but I also thought how cool it
would be if I could be the one doing the hosting, looking
after people that way, making them feel happy. I'd say
that night out changed my life.

I always wanted to go to clubs and after the clubs I
always wanted to go to house parties. Even then, it
wasn't exciting enough. To me, house parties with just

a loud stereo on were boring, so I bought a twister and a strobe and the next time I went out I stuffed them in my rucksack. I went to a club and danced loads all night. Then, just as they were shutting down, I danced my way to the cloakroom, got hold of my rucksack, opened it up in front of everyone and shouted, 'Party! I've got the lights, come on!' And off we would go, all through the night.

Later, when I got my first car, I took this up a level by packing my full set of decks in the back as well as speakers, records and my usual lights. The minute a club was over, as long as we could find a house or venue, we would set up a near-perfect nightclub system within about fifty minutes. Every week we would turn someone's kitchen or sitting room into the best late-night club in Dublin. Looking back, I can see now that I was effectively running parties and setting up 'mobile' nightclubs already, but back then I never saw it that way – it was just that I just didn't want the party to end.

By then I had progressed quite a bit as a DJ, so I saved up for months and bought myself a set of Technics, which for me was like buying a Rolls-Royce (I have twelve sets now – if only I'd known back then). They cost £1,200 – a fortune. I bought them on hire purchase but, just as I was about to go out of the door and collect them, me ma and da sat me down and said, 'Listen Fran, this is a lot of money.'

'But Da,' I said, 'it's me future!'

'Fran! Come on,' he replied.

'Listen, I am going to be a DJ and I am going to make money off these, I am investing in my future.'

He was still chuckling at me when I left the house, but I knew deep down that both he and Ma could see I wasn't messing about and they backed me all the way. Later, when I said I wanted to take a sound-engineering course, they were both fully behind me. I'd got pretty good on the turntables but I wanted to get into music so badly that I was keen to expand my knowledge, to learn as much as I could. I saw this course and thought it would give me another string to my bow other just than DJ-ing.

Dance music was everywhere at the time, so if I was able to learn these engineering skills I thought I might be able to break into music through that avenue. I went there three evenings a week to study and absolutely loved the practical side of things, using the computers, learning sequencing, all that aspect of it. Just as at school, I found the theoretical side of it very hard, so I didn't really do too well there – in fact, I failed all the papers. I was fascinated with being in the studio, though, and I was actually really good on the equipment.

When the course finished, I used to go back to the college and show the new students how to use all the gear; I just loved being around it all. In exchange for helping out with the new students they gave me free studio time and I eventually ended up doing a few sessions for adverts and other work. I didn't care what I was working on, really, as long as I was playing music, writing music, living music.

# CHAPTER FIVE

# FLOW

When I was 16, I opened my first nightclub. I'd left school with those six certificates but had no interest in taking my education any further – at least not the kind of education you got in schools and colleges. With all the DJ-ing and hosting I was doing anyway, I had got to know loads of people in and around Dublin, so it just felt completely natural for me to set up my own club. Looking back, I was still a child, but at the time it was just the obvious next step.

The club was called Flow. I'd been looking for a venue for a while, searching all over the place. One of the guys who worked at my dad's video shop was a doorman in Leeson Street, one of Dublin's main club and bar areas. He mentioned that there was a basement available next to where he worked. In the day it was a Rape Crisis Centre, but at night unused.

I quickly arranged an appointment with the man who ran the RCC and turned up for the meeting bang on time.

I introduced myself and told him that I wanted to put on these parties. To his credit, he said, 'Oh, brilliant idea!' I was surprised, I was just a kid and yet he went with it straight away.

'Would some of our people be able to come to these parties?' he said.

'Of course!'

At this point, he didn't realise that I was going to open at 2am and close at 8am! I called up my cousin Owen, who is very good at organising things and has a great business head, and we started getting the venue ready for the first night. We flyered everywhere and got all the equipment ready.

The deal was that I paid the RCC guy rent for the lease and he gave me Friday, Saturday and Sunday to use the building. Actually, I only used one of the nights, doing a different style of night each week. We had no licences, nothing. We just got a gaff and said it was for 'private parties'. But that didn't stop us selling alcohol out of the back cloakroom. Without a licence it was illegal, so what we did was send people to the front bar to buy a soft drink, then give them a drinks ticket, which they would then take to the back cloakroom, where we would pour an alcoholic drink into their glass. It was all very crafty and helped, on reflection, by the tenacity of my youth.

Perhaps not surprisingly, the very first night, mainly friends and a few punters, was actually not that busy. But the problem was we made the mistake of opening from 11pm to 4am, which was absolutely stupid because it meant we were competing with massive clubs down the street and no one is going to come to a new, small club, given the choice. That's why I came up with the idea of opening at 2am and closing at 8am in the morning.

We'd been partying pretty hard at places like Déjà Vu, which was underneath a restaurant owned by my dad. That's when I started getting really good at hosting and DJ-ing, using my own decks, getting everything together. There were a few of us who worked at Flow: a guy called Nigel, a friend of mine, Jamie and a handful of others. At this stage everyone in Ireland was playing house music so that's what we chose to go along with, for the time being.

We were very good at putting the word about and the people who did come to Flow loved it. Within two weeks of the club opening, we had queues around the block. It got to the point where punters were jamming the road. The police were coming over and asking, 'What the hell is going on?' not least because this went on until 8am each morning. Of course, the other bars and clubs in the area were not happy. A lot of them were private-membership clubs as well as late-night bars, but all of them shut by about 2am or 3am. Nonetheless, local opposition was fierce; the other clubs went mental. It wasn't so much that we were competition, they just didn't want any more attention being brought on to the street than there already was.

They got us closed down eventually, after the first summer. The police raided the place, went through everything at the club and even searched through our houses. They couldn't do a lot except shut us down, which they did with a stern warning of 'Learn your lesson, don't do it again.'

I had learnt a lot of lessons with Flow at Leeson Street, actually, but I don't think they were the same ones that the police were talking about. What an experience for me! It certainly helped my confidence a little – when I'd left school, they'd all told me, 'You will make nothing of yourself', yet within six months I had opened my first club. Me ma spoke with one of my old teachers a few months after I left and he said, 'So what's he doing now?' probably expecting me to be on the dole or doing some menial job. 'Oh, Fran owns a nightclub in Leeson Street,' she replied.

I suppose the variety of jobs my parents took when I was young must have had an effect on me, in that I knew neither of them was 'clocking-in', yet we were getting by. It made me think there were different ways to earn a living. Ma and Da worked so hard to keep us well fed and looked after. Mom was mainly a housewife but she had a fashion thing going on with clothes and jewellery – women from the estate would come around and buy stuff. She had a shop up the road from my dad's shop too, where she'd sell the fashion stuff, but she put so much energy and love into being a housewife. With Da at work so much, I spent a lot of time with me ma and with my other brother as well she had her hands full! If I had problems when I was little, I often spoke to me ma first.

As a jack of all trades, *master* of all trades, me da did so many jobs when I was young. To the eternal credit of me ma and da, the three of us never worried about food and being looked after, because we knew inside that they would always do whatever it took to keep us safe, warm and fed. It was hard for them, but they never faltered. As I have said, my dad was the first person to open a 24-hour video shop in Ireland. Well, I remember when he went to England and came back with all these boxes full of tapes. That night I spent hours sitting in the living room sifting through all these boxes, flicking open the video cases, ecstatic at what might be on these films. I always loved watching movies, possibly because I understood everything that was going on in them – unlike at school.

I was bang into me da's shop, it was great at that age to have your dad owning a video shop – you got to see all the films before they came out. I loved it. I thought my dad had the best job in the world; I remember thinking, *My Dad knows the story, he knows everything.*

Inevitably perhaps, given my fascination with films, I started off part-time at my dad's video shop then ended up working full shifts as I grew older and wanted to earn more money. When I was 16 I was making £300 a week working for me da in those video shops. I worked five or so twelve-hour shifts a week, but I was always out partying as well. I would never say this to my own son, but it is a fact that my education came from watching movies. I loved the job in Dad's shop not just because films are my obsession but also because the shop became a social club for all my mates. We'd all meet up there before heading out to town or just to hang around. It was brilliant.

When the Kevin Costner/Whitney Houston hit movie *Bodyguard* came out, my dad got hold of a promotional jacket with the film's title across the back, which I wore loads. This wasn't because I had designs on being a bodyguard myself – I'll be honest, the thought had never crossed my mind and besides, what are the chances of growing up in Tallaght, near Dublin and ending up being a bodyguard for famous celebrities?

I soon got enough money together to think about getting a place of my own. Myself and some friends found a four-bedroom house to rent in Taylor's Row, Rathfarnham, some eight miles from my parents' house. When I told me ma and da they were shocked, but by now I'd just got my first car so this detached house seemed like the next logical step. To start off with we had no furniture and the only things I took there apart from my clothes were my decks.

This gaff changed people.

There was a lot of partying going on in the house. Jerry and myself were working our bollocks off and on a night we would come home and there'd already be around forty people in our front room dancing. Mental! However, a lot of strange things went on in that house. It was the first time that I experienced the feeling that someone was around, even though I couldn't see anyone. I would regularly wake up thinking that someone was standing looking over me, even though no one was there – and when I did, I was always incredibly cold, even in the summer. Weird shit. It felt like being in that movie, *Stand By Me*.

No doubt about it, there was a sinister side to Taylor's Row. Strange things happened there. I was convinced that someone had died there in some strange way, because there was the weirdest atmosphere; I never wanted to be in the house on my own. One night, a mate got so drunk on wine that he set his own room on fire, with him still in it. The windows were open and the curtains were blowing about and caught on the fire. I was in my room, smelled the burning and kicked the door in. I picked him up on my shoulder, dumped him in the sitting room, put the fire out and went back to my room.

Maybe that was just down to the drink. But one particular night something happened that was down to way more than that. I was away from the house that night and my housemates were having a party, so I was gutted that I was going to miss it. It was a massive night, and got the neighbours so mad that they pulled the electric supply out. However, when I came back the next morning, something very strange had obviously gone on. My mates all looked glazed over. That night destroyed about ten people's lives, including the lives of my five best mates at the time. One of them is in a mental home; one of them *never* sleeps at night or when it is dark;

another one became a raving alcoholic soon afterwards. I have sat up many nights with the friend, who cannot sleep in the dark, waiting for him to doze off, but he never does until daybreak and the sun comes out. Then he is asleep within seconds. It's awful.

There were probably bad drugs involved that night, but that was not unusual. Something else had gone on. One thing I do know for a fact is that whatever happened to my friends that night, they were never the same. Maybe it was haunted – I never found out what it was, but I feel very fortunate that I wasn't in the house at the time. I truly believe the reason I was away was because in the whole blueprint of life, I wasn't meant to be there.

I'll be honest with you: there are not a lot of things that I deeply regret in my life. But one mistake I made in particular does stand out and it is to do with my granddad. When I was about 17 we were at a wedding. Now, my granddad was a big old drinker, a larger-than-life character, the centre of any party. What a mentaller he was – I can see him sitting in his couch drinking his shandies as clear as yesterday. He'd owned all these supermarkets and had a really successful business, which in turn had lead to Ma meeting Da. He'd also owned a delicatessen selling fresh chickens and done loads of different stuff. He was one of these characters who made it then lost it, then made it again.

Jesus, he was a proper funny old geezer and everyone loved him. He'd looked after us a lot when we were kids and I loved him to bits.

Anyway, he was pissed at this party and was messing around with my girlfriend, trying to kiss her. Smack! I stuck one on him. As if that wasn't bad enough, I refused to speak to him for weeks afterwards. The problem was that was the last time I ever spoke to him, as he passed away two months later. I didn't even go to the hospital to give him my respects. It was terrible. I was so young and ignorant to the complexities of life – I behaved like a child. It was stupid. I deeply regret all of that and I can never put it right. If there is any one thing I could go back and change, that is it. Later, when I realised how daft I had been, I went to visit his grave, but all I could do was talk to him, although it did help relieve some of the awful guilt I felt about what had happened. Now I never leave a fight to fester and I always tell me ma and da I love them when I speak to them. That was a very hard lesson.

It was particularly sad because at the time everything else in my life was going really well. I had good money coming in for my age, I was partying all the time, I had a good job that I enjoyed and lived with a load of mates in this big house. Then, to top it all, I hooked up with my first serious girlfriend, Emma.

It's weird how things work out in life. Remember that guy Nick that I had my first fight with? Well, Emma was going out with him when I met her. And the very first time I was introduced to her was pretty strange too. I walked into the house in Taylor's Row and Nick was there with Emma. As soon as I saw them, I had this sudden thought: *Oh my God, I am going to be with her!* I've only ever had it twice, with Emma and with my fiancée Tash. There was something instantaneous about the chemistry with Emma but she was with Nick, so that was that. Initially it wasn't even the way she looked that attracted me – there was just something about her.

The first time I was with Emma, we were all sitting in a pub and Nick was with her. We all quite liked Emma. Later, we all moved on to a club and then I had to leave to do some DJ-ing. As I was getting my stuff together, Emma turned to me and said, 'Can I come with you?'

I said, 'I don't know, you know, Nick and everything...'

I asked my friend Jerry what he thought, but he said, 'I don't know' as well, so it was all a little bit awkward. We packed all our stuff in the car and then as we jumped in the back, Emma did too. Just at that minute, Nick came out of the club and shouted after her. I looked at her and asked, 'Shall I go?' she replied, 'Yes' so I said, 'Drive!' and we headed off with Nick's bird in the back of our car.

She came back to my gaff and we spent the whole night together chatting. I just totally fell in love with her right there and then. I remember sitting there and telling her, 'I want to own a nightclub'; we were both talking about our dreams, it was so easy and natural. She listened to everything I had to say and I wanted to hear what she had to say too. And when I said, 'I am not just going to run a nightclub, I am going to own one,' she never doubted me for one second.

We were together for three years from that night. She got to know my parents really well and me ma treated her like a daughter. Ma saw her in Dublin in 2005 and says she still loves her – they were very close. Emma was a constant factor in my life from the age of 16 to 19.

I am always attracted to mentallers and Emma could party with the best of them. We had some wild times. Strangely, when I had first met her I hadn't noticed her looks but after a while I thought to myself, 'Woah! She is beautiful.' By then, I was head over heels. Unfortunately, we started having fights and some of them were bad-ass fights. We'd moved in to an apartment quite soon after hooking up together and where we lived, there was a great big driveway and our flat was the first one you could see. I came home after one big fight to find Emma throwing all my records out of the windows. I could hear the vinyl smashing as it hit the ground. I was furious! I ran upstairs and we had another big fight.

Sadly, after we'd lived together for two years, we eventually decided to go our separate ways. It was a little more complicated than your usual boyfriend/girlfriend relationship because we were sharing this flat. However, I have to admit that when we both moved out of the apartment, I moved straight back in the same day. She was fuming!

We actually got back together a short while later but the rot had set in and it wasn't to last. We were both very young and she'd done some travelling on her own while we were going out, which created a gap between us. It was hard to know what to do to get closer together and when I eventually realised it was over, the decision to walk away was unbelievably hard to make.

When I broke up with Emma, the pain I went through was crippling. I spoke for ages with me da about it but I could not be consoled; I was devastated. What made it worse was the fact that, as in the song lyric, in the twist of separation she excelled at being free. She was out with her mates, drinking, partying, apparently having a great time, yet I missed her so much I just couldn't move on. The night after we broke up she was sitting in a restaurant over the road arm in arm with a bloke. Even though we were no longer together, I was just horrified. I can't speak for Emma, but I think she was hurt too.

After we broke up, I lost it. I went out every day to distract myself – I hated sitting at home mulling over what had happened and what might happen next. I couldn't stop thinking where she was, who she was with, what she was doing, what time she was out until enjoying herself. One night I went clubbing at The System with my friend Barry. My phone was switched off and Emma had tried to call me but wasn't getting through, so she phoned Barry about ten times instead. He saw her name come up and just didn't take the call – he thought I was better off away from all that. Then I went to use his phone the next morning and there were all these missed calls from Emma, I was fuming! I knew we couldn't be together, but at the time I was going through that raw phase just after a break-up when you are utterly confused and upset.

I actually saw Emma a couple of months ago for the first time in years. I'd just come back from the jungle and was in the local pub with a suit on and a big, funky beard. My mom brought this girl over and said, 'Do you know who this is?' and I admitted that I didn't. She said, 'It's Emma!' Even after everything that's happened, we still had that little spark – I guess it will always be there with someone you've spent so much time with. Back then, though, the hurt of the break-up seemed to last *forever*. I think in a way the disintegration of that relationship closed me off to feeling anything for anyone else for a long time. I wasn't interested in being with anyone for ages.

# CHAPTER SIX

# THE WATCHER

Although you might think I was brimming with self-belief as a youngster, at this stage in my teens I still wasn't really that confident in myself. Yet at the age of 17 I got my first job working on a nightclub door. To trace this back you have to rewind about three years to one incident in particular that highlighted my lack of self-confidence but also proved to be the trigger for me to get into weight-training and gym work. I was out one night in a club called The Kitchen and these two English blokes were chatting up me bird and giving it loads. I didn't like it, but they were big lads and when I said something about it, one of them smacked me in the head – he caught me a classic and knocked me flat on my arse.

I felt shit that I couldn't stand up for myself, it really upset me. The very next morning I got up and said, 'That's it!' and I started training. At first, as I've mentioned, I used weights in our garage and often worked out with my dad. Then, when I really got into it,

I joined a local gym and started to get serious. I went from eleven and a half stone to fifteen stone in four months. I ate everything I could, fourteen eggs for breakfast, ten slices of ham, I was like Mr Strong! I actually ate quite badly sometimes because I would eat chocolate just to put on weight even though chocolate is not good fat. But I was getting bigger, much bigger. If someone hadn't seen me for a few weeks, they would be like 'Jesus!' when they saw me again. That's how it started and how I got big enough to get into security and the door work. In many ways, it was the best thing I ever did because my confidence really started to grow as a result. I got into really good shape, I was looking good and I liked looking good, which in turn made me start to feel better about myself.

The first door work I got was at a club called Night Owls in Dublin, which was seriously rough. My friend Colin – we called him 'Loaf' because he had a deadly head butt on him, a total legend – said to the club owner, 'Me mate Fran wants a job, he's a good scrapper' and so I got the nod. Loaf was working at The Kitchen, one of the city's highest-profile clubs and the place where I'd been humiliated by those two men chatting me bird up, so it was great that he put in a word for me. You didn't need a licence to work doors in Ireland then and at Night Owls being a good scrapper was qualification enough.

I didn't want to tell me ma what I was doing for work, so on my first night I got ready in my room behind closed doors. I had my Tin-Tin haircut and was all tanned up, wearing black trousers, a white shirt and dickie bow. As I crept out of the house, Ma saw me and said, 'Ah! You're not a bloody stripper, are you?'

All the old lads on the door of Night Owls were knackers. Some of them had worked in that environment for years, so it was no wonder. At first they called me 'pretty boy' – 'Look at you, pretty boy, you won't have that face left on you in a few weeks' time!'

That first night I worked at Night Owls someone got stabbed.

We used to stand on boxes positioned all around the club and if someone spotted a fight, we'd radio through saying 'Red card, red card! Middle stage!' Then you'd see twenty massive bouncers steaming in through the crowds, knocking people over and smacking punters all over the gaff. The first night I went home exhausted from scrapping, I could barely stand. It was mental.

On reflection, though, it was great that Night Owls was so rough, because it got me to thinking about better ways of doing the job and, indeed, a club in general. I did have plenty of scraps, don't get me wrong, but I was also good at talking to people as well, and I began to learn how to avoid a fight rather than just win one. I always knew I had a skill for talking to people. To this day, this remains one of my biggest strengths in terms of door or security work.

It was also my first experience of the attitude of women to bouncers – at least in that part of town, anyway. Birds would come into the club and the veteran doormen would be chatting them up, talking to their tits and shagging them in the toilets. I don't know what it was, probably the alcohol and the excitement of the night out, but the women there would throw themselves at us, chatting us up constantly all night long. I had always done OK with birds, but this was full on. I didn't pay attention to it, it was all drink, everyone was pissed – and let's face it, that's not very attractive is it? But I did watch the doormen and the punters and think to myself, *I am going to be really good at this.*

This inkling that I could be so much better on the door than the people I was watching was reinforced one night when I went to a club in Dublin called The System. I walked up to the door and this big, stocky doorman was shamelessly flirting with my bird. I was standing there, smaller than him, feeling terrible but also looking at this bloke thinking it could be done with so much more class. He was staring down at me and making me feel insecure but I had been in that position at school when I was bullied – it was nothing new, just a different environment. I knew he had no idea how bad he was making me feel; I also knew I could do that job and make people feel *good*.

The next night at Night Owls I started to put a few things I'd learned into practice. When people walked up to me, I would say to the bloke, 'You look wicked! How are you doing?' I would of course say hello to the girl, but I would always look the man in the face, pay him attention and not make him feel threatened. I enjoyed doing it and it seemed to work.

I was only a kid really – albeit a big one at about sixteen stone – but I really enjoyed working that door. I worked from 11pm to 3am, only four or five hours and yet we were paid the same as people were getting for a nine-hour shift. Fair enough, we'd be scrapping for most of those five hours with people who'd often think nothing of pulling a knife, smashing a glass in your face or kicking you in the head. But when the shift was over, I could spend all day sitting at home relaxing, working out in the gym, knowing that I didn't have to go to work until 10.30pm. One of my mate Barry's girlfriends had given him a sun-bed. His parents wouldn't let him keep it in his house, so we had it in ours, and naturally enough I started using it. I went from being pasty white to sunburned in about forty-eight hours.

I really enjoyed that period, I got into a great routine and it introduced me to a job and lifestyle that meant I met tons of people every night. Pretty soon I knew everybody in town. I started to realise I actually had leadership skills and was able to direct people, make the right decisions, make the right moves in a split second. It's just a life-awareness thing, following my gut instincts. To me, one of the most appealing aspects of door work has always been the feeling of being in control of something that is by definition out of control.

But at Night Owls I had plenty of chances to put all my doorman theories into practice, let me tell you! The first big fight I was involved in started when a guy on the door was grabbed from the steps by eight blokes and they all began scrapping in the street. Then passers-by started piling in too. It was mayhem! When I ran out on the street, the first thing I saw was one of our guys with six blokes kicking his head.

That night there was just three of us working, with twelve people attacking us. We all piled in and I was being smacked around but getting off all right, for some reason. At one point, this little bloke came at me so I grabbed him in a headlock, lifted him off the ground and rammed him into this mob of people fighting. I noticed they were punching at him, their own mate, to try to get to me, so that gave me an idea.

I wrapped my arms around him while still keeping this headlock and effectively turned this weedy little prick into a shield. I waded into the crowd with him thrust out in front of me and I was swinging him around like a weapon. He was too small to stop me, but perhaps he should have thought of that before he had a go. Bad call!

The doorman they'd first started on was still getting kicked around, so keeping hold of this little bloke – who was wriggling like a snake to get free – I went down on one knee to help my colleague. Once he was on his feet again he would be able to sort himself out, but if you are being kicked in the head when you are down it is hard to stand up.

I was at knee level now and all these blokes were kicking and punching at me, some even had sticks and rocks, but nothing was hitting me, they were just pummelling their own mate. He was taking a right beating. I was even blocking punches with him – he was really very useful! I managed to drag the doorman to his feet and pushed him towards the door of Night Owls and safety but, as I did, I realised that now I was out in the dark street entirely on my own, a few feet from this baying mob. In a second, they all turned their focus on me. I thought I was fucked.

I started walking backwards towards the door, still using this bloke as a shield, but it was getting pretty difficult. As I tried to walk up the club steps, I stumbled and sensed that events were finally overtaking me. Just then, I felt some big hands grab my shoulders and I knew my colleagues were about to pull me out of the danger. So, with one last effort, I stood up and threw this little prick in the air. He came crashing down on top of his mates. We got back to the sanctuary of Night Owls – if it could ever really be called 'sanctuary' – and took a collective sigh of relief. One doorman had broken a bone so badly that it was sticking out of his arm through the skin. It was a serious injury, with blood pouring out. Then we discovered that a new doorman had seen our guy getting a kicking but hadn't radioed for help, which was a serious breach of trust for doormen, so someone smashed him in the face.

Night Owls was one of the toughest clubs in Dublin, and some nights were crammed with fights and dangerous situations, but I loved every minute of it –

there couldn't have been a better experience to start off my career as a doorman.

———

After I had been working doors for a while, I began to get really big. I used to train every day. Back then I was really clueless about how to train properly, the correct diet, the way to use the equipment, but to be fair I was just starting out. That's why I ended up doing a personal-training course. My mom and dad were getting really worried about me because I was working the door and they were like, 'You need to do something, you have to have something to fall back on, you can't be doing the doors for the rest of your life. You don't need the hassle. You need something more secure.' My parents have been so patient with me over the years. I was always thinking about things I wanted to do, but so often I would never actually put the work in. They never scoffed at me, they were always encouraging but eventually they told me, 'You know what? You've got to do it yourself, off your own back, we can't be forcing you to do it all the time.'

And they were right. Working on doors isn't an ideal life job, even though it can work for some people who never do anything different. So I did this personal-training course and that opened up jobs such as working as a trainer in gyms – plus, it also meant I was training properly myself, so it was well worthwhile. Besides, in my mind I never wanted to spend the rest of my life working doors, so something that might take me away from that was very welcome.

My life really began changing the day I began travelling. I say 'travelling', but I'm specifically thinking of a trip to Greece with the lads when I was 19. I was working really hard at this point, doing three jobs at the same time. If my shifts didn't work out right I would work the door on one club until the early morning, then I'd get home and grab a couple of hours' kip, before heading back out to start the early-bird shift at the gym where I was working as a personal trainer. Then, if I was lucky I'd eat something before donning the black suit again and heading off to another club. I was getting a handful of hours' sleep each night but I really wanted to get some money behind me so I just kept putting in the hours. I had also moved back in with my mom and dad for a year to try to save more. I liked my creature comforts and, up until this point at least, had not been very adventurous in terms of travel.

One day I was working at the gym when my mobile rang. It was a mate: 'We're going on a lads' holiday, you fancy coming?' I really fancied a break, so I turned to my manageress and asked, 'Can I get two weeks off?' And she replied, 'No way!'

What I did next was a spur-of-the-moment thing, but looking back it was a watershed moment in my life. I thought, *Hang on a minute*, took a coin out of my pocket, then flipped it in the air. Heads was travel and leave Ireland behind, unbeknown to me at the time opening up a life I could only have dreamed of working in that small-town gym.

The coin landed in my palm.

Heads it was.

'I'm really sorry, I have to do this. I have to go on this holiday even if it costs me my job,' I told the manageress.

That 'heads' changed my entire life.

# CHAPTER SEVEN

# THE ACCIDENTAL TOURIST

As soon as I had decided to go travelling, something inside me just clicked and I suddenly experienced a resilience I'd never felt before. I don't know why that was, but I simply felt stronger inside. Maybe because a whole new world was opening up in front of me, I'm not sure, but what I do know is that from that moment flipping the coin in the gym, I was never the same again.

I'd been on a few holidays with my parents when I was young – Lanzarote and stuff like that – and I'd also been to Majorca with Emma, but I hadn't really done that much travelling. The lads' holiday was hardly a round-the-world jaunt – we went to Kos in Greece – but it opened up the floodgates that would lead to me landing in London and my life being completely transformed.

Back then, the attraction was simply to get away, relax, train a little and enjoy myself. At that point I hadn't been drinking for about a year and a half – occasionally I'd have a few, but nothing much. But unlike a lot of the lads, I wasn't going out there for the booze. We landed in Kos, got off the plane and were herded onto the transfer bus with about eighty other holiday-makers. Like anyone else, you always hope you're not the last people on the bus to be dropped off. Well, I kid you not, this bloody bus drove around Kos all day long and we were sweating like pigs and bored out of our minds. Then, when we finally got to our drop-off – and yes, we *were* the last ones – the hotel looked like a right shithole.

Fortunately, it turned out that the owner of the hotel was an Aussie and was a sound bloke, so we ended up being really pleased with it. Unfortunately, tensions started to develop pretty quickly between myself and the rest of the lads. We even argued when we got off the bus that morning at the start of the holiday. The problem was that everyone except me was on a proper, full-on lads' holiday. The very first night we went out I wasn't drinking and all the lads were calling me a boring bastard!

At that point I just wasn't in the mood for drinking, it felt good not to. Instead, I went to the gym and trained, finally managed to get some rest and just started to relax from all the hard work back home. The owner of the local gym had a security company too and it happened to be the one mainly used by the resort's bouncers. Within a day or so, I knew all the doormen on the island. The lads couldn't believe it when we went to a club called Fashion – I walked up and the doorman was like, 'Hey,

Fran!' We'd been there less than a day. So when I did go out with the lads, we were getting into clubs for free and drinking free booze all night.

Although I got a buzz out of largely being by myself that holiday, we did have some funny times. One night my best friend and I were coming out of a club with this bird he'd pulled. He said he wanted to shag her but could only get two people on his moped, so he promised he'd drop her off at her room first and then come back for me.

I waited for forty minutes but the bastard never came back. It was an hour's walk back to the hotel and I was fuming, absolutely fuming. On the way back I passed by the apartment block where I knew this girl was staying and I saw a moped that looked like his outside the place. I went up to her room, knocked on the door and dragged him outside. When I'd finished arguing with him, I walked back outside and saw the moped standing by the swimming pool, so I threw it in. It turned out my mate was driving someone else's moped, so it wasn't even his! I continued my walk back but just outside the apartment block there were a few more mopeds, so I kicked them all over just in case one of them was actually his. I was livid!

As the holiday went on I found myself gradually falling out with the lads, and by the time I got back on the plane I wasn't speaking to anyone. It was the longest plane flight ever. We got back and went our separate ways and I didn't speak to them for a while.

However, on the very last night of that holiday, I met a Danish pop star. I kid you not, I was just standing outside a bar when this Danish bird comes up to me – beautiful she was. I had broken up with Emma over a year before yet I still wasn't in the mood for relationships; my head was still a bit wrecked by all that. That's partly why I hadn't been interested in the booze-and-birds holiday the lads were after.

Anyway, this Danish girl came over and said, 'Hi, how you doing?' *Jesus*, I thought to myself, *she is fit!* We started chatting and when I asked her what she did for a living, she said, 'I am a pop star.' I thought, *Yeah! Whatever!* After all, when you are on holiday, most lads are racing drivers or fighter pilots or whatever. But she was really nice and we had a good old chat.

Then she said, 'Come over and have a drink with me later,' and I replied, 'Yeah, I might do, very nice to meet you.'

About half an hour later, her friend came over and asked, 'What's going on? Why aren't you coming over to join us?' And I said, 'Well, you know...' This 'pop star' eventually came over and got me to join them, telling me I was the first person who hadn't chatted her up or paid her too much attention. Again she mentioned that she was in a band, but I still didn't take it seriously.

We spent a wicked night together, absolutely wicked. We went down and watched the sun come up on the beach, then had breakfast first thing in the morning. It was lovely. She was leaving the very next day, so I dropped her back to her hotel. I was surprised when she said she wanted to change her flights so we could get to know each other a little better, but as it happened she was unable to. I gave her my telephone number and said, 'I'm sure we'll see each other again some time,' like you do.

However, when I got back to my hotel, I found myself feeling really sad that she was leaving so I decided to go and find her. Me and a mate jumped on his moped and went to track her down. I rang the number she had given me, but it was the first time I had rung an international phone so I was dialling the wrong digits, and couldn't get through. Eventually, I found her hotel; she was in reception getting ready to leave. When she saw me, she dropped her suitcases and hugged me and we agreed to stay in touch. I told her I would be back home soon and to give me a ring.

I'd been back in Dublin a day or so when the phone rang and it was this Danish bird. She said she wanted to come and see me and had booked a flight for the very next day! I was a little shocked but looking forward to seeing her. I told my dad the story and was laughing, saying, 'There's no way she is a pop star, but it's a good line.' The next morning I got up to go to the toilet and when I came back there was a photograph of this girl pinned to my bedroom door – complete with confirmation that she was indeed a very famous Danish pop star.

'She is who she says she is, Fran!' said my dad when I got downstairs. He'd been on the internet and was laughing out loud.

It turned out her band was really big news in Europe. I still didn't really give a shit, though, to be honest – I just thought she was a lovely girl. Anyway, she came over to Ireland and spent a great week there but then when it was time to go home she said, 'Come back to Denmark with me.' By now I had spent most of my savings, but I fancied seeing Denmark so I kept working, got some cash together, then booked a flight.

When I got to her place, it was a huge, beautiful penthouse overlooking the city of Copenhagen. On just my second night there, we went to see The Eurythmics (my dad was always a big fan and so was I). After the concert I found myself sitting there with Annie Lennox, Dave Stewart and some of The Spice Girls, just having a completely normal chat. The legendary pop manager Simon Fuller came over and looked at me, then said, 'You look quite good, can you sing?' and I was like, *Who the hell is that?* 'Yeah,' I told him, 'but only in the shower.' I didn't have a clue who he was – it was the first time I had been around celebrities like that, but it didn't bother me, it wasn't something I looked up to. I just got on really well with them and they were wicked artists having a normal chat, a good night.

I fell into a bit of a routine: I would go to Denmark for a few weeks, then come back to Dublin, work a load of shifts and get some cash together then fly out to see the Danish girl again. When I stood on the door at these rough Dublin clubs telling the lads what I was doing and who I was spending time with, they were like, 'Are you taking the piss?' We even had a short break in London one time, my first visit to the capital city that would soon play such a major part in my life. The hotel I stayed at with her would later be the same place where I had one of my first kisses with Tash. My first experience of London was walking out of the Copthorne Hotel into Kensington High Street. That night I went into the West End for a Chinese and couldn't believe my eyes. I loved it from the very first second. I thought, *This place is deadly!* I don't know why but I was immediately drawn towards London. We would meet again...

I was already getting itchy feet through travelling back and forth to Denmark plus certain aspects of my life in Dublin were not very enjoyable any more. One incident at a trendy bar called The Bailey proved to be pivotal in my eventual decision to move away. I was working there one night when a drug addict attacked me. I took him outside but he went at me again in the street and tried to stick a cigarette in my face. Although I got out of the way, he was relentless and went to headbutt me. I side-stepped that and thought it was finished, so I turned to walk back inside, but he came charging after me again and punched me from behind, then ran off across the road into another pub.

I went after him because he was causing a lot of trouble. When I found him, I swept his legs out from under him and he rolled over and knocked a heater on top of himself. That gave myself and this other doorman a chance to get hold of him and... let's just say, try to calm him down.

Things started to get out of hand, though. A third doorman came in, thought I was out of control and took a swing at me, hitting me on the shoulder. He turned to leave and grabbed a hold of the pub door handles but just as he did I swept his legs and pulled him back towards me so hard he actually pulled the door handles off with him. It was a scene and a half – to be fair to the other doormen they were just trying to calm me down, they didn't know how it had all started. It was a real mess. Eventually the druggie got a smack and ran off. Then he came back, claiming I had attacked him and all that. The security company wanted to speak to me about it, but I was off to Denmark the next morning for a few weeks so they never got their chat.

When I came back, though, there was murder about it. This all added to a growing feeling within me that it was time I left Dublin and looked for new challenges somewhere else. I could sense matters were coming to a head. I had been off rampaging in Denmark, spending all my savings living in this massive penthouse. One morning I woke up and thought, *This isn't working any more.* I have to admit the doubt was compounded by the fact that I was still madly in love with Emma; even after all that time I couldn't stop thinking about her. I was still messed up in the head, so I couldn't fully involve myself in a new relationship. I tried to leave on a couple of occasions and one morning my Danish girlfriend even caught me packing. I knew I had to go, so one morning I got a cab to the airport and that was that, see you later.

I arrived back in Dublin and me mate Lar, who used to work with me at The Bailey, rang me up. He'd only just got back from spending some time in Spain himself and wanted to try to hook up with an ex-girlfriend in London. I'd literally come back from Denmark the previous evening but Lar didn't know this, so it was very lucky he caught me at home. By then I'd spoken a few times with various mates about moving away from Dublin. I recall one time with my friend Barry – we were heading into town in a cab and I turned to him and said, 'Mate, we have got to do something special, I don't know what but I am going to do something.' Whenever I had these chats, London was always the preferred choice of destination. None of us knew anyone in that capital but it just seemed like the most exciting place to move to.

'So do you fancy moving to England with me tomorrow then or what?' asked Lar.

Although we'd spoken about it, the sudden prospect of moving to London was a bolt out of the blue.

I thought about my situation: I'd sold my car, spent most of my money, I was tired of some of the door work and complications such as what had happened at The Bailey, I'd got the travel bug and I wanted a new challenge.

'Lar, yes, why not?'

We tried to get tickets for the next day but with no joy so we ended up flying out to London the day after that. I had £180 and a one-way ticket in my pocket, plus a sports bag over my shoulder with a few pairs of black trousers and T-shirts inside.

I was on my way to London.

---

I flew over to England with Lar and this internet expert, who I called 'www.Ken'. His ma and da were a pilot and air hostess for Aer Lingus, I think. Ken didn't really know why he came, I think it was mainly because Lar dragged him over! I didn't know him before our trip – the first time I ever met Ken was when we walked into the airport and saw the two of them queuing for our flight.

I was so excited. We got on the plane and I punched the air and shouted, 'Come on!' I was so convinced this was going to be the best adventure ever. I kept pressing the button to call the air hostesses and the girls were all laughing and enjoying the attention, but I could see Ken getting wound up and eventually he said, 'Stop doing that, will you – have some respect for them!' I thought, *Uh-oh!* The strange thing is, when Lar and Ken came over to London, they were the straightest blokes in the universe, but it wasn't long before they turned into lunatics (and unfortunately, Lar didn't manage to get back with the girlfriend he was looking for).

We walked out of King's Cross train station with a rucksack each, no return plane ticket and very little money. I'd spent £20 on a cab to the airport so all I had now was £160.

*Top*: June 1978 and trials for *I'm Not A Celebrity Yet! Get Me Out Of Here!*

*Right*: My da (Dermot), me and my little brother Gerry.

*Top*: I was four months old when this was taken in April 1978.

*Bottom*: A summer holiday in 1982. My brother Gerry was two then and I was four. My ma Betty is sitting between us.

Me playing on my skateboard in the spring of 1989.

*Top*: Left to right: Adam, my youngest brother, when he was just over one-and-a-half, m⟨
and my brother Gerry.

*Bottom*: Me and Gerry in 1986.

*Top*: Me at 13 in 1989 with my ma.

*Bottom*: I was always interested in music! Here I am in 1987 brushing up on my keyboard skills.

Me with Kian from Westlife at Brown's in early 2003.

uckering up with Westlife's Brian.

Mylene Klass and me at a party in 2004.

With nowhere to stay.

And no job.

And no food.

It was a little bit freaky, I have to say.

That first night we had no choice but to stay in a bed and breakfast, which cost us £40 each, so a huge chunk of my spare cash had gone within twenty-four hours. The easiest way out of our predicament was to get work and both Lar and me had thought we could just fly over and start working the doors in London's clubland. Wrong! We soon discovered you had to be licensed to work doors in England. This meant you needed to get a security badge to work at any club in town. To get the badge you had to attend a three-day course and then it was probably a four-to-eight week wait until the badge was officially awarded. Oh my God! Disaster!

We were gutted. What were we supposed to do now? I had £120 in my pocket. So the next day it was vital that we found somewhere more affordable to stay. We started scouring the estate agents' windows in King's Cross. It just so happened that as we were peering into this one window, a Russian guy came up to us and said, 'I think I know where we can stay, this place, it's called the Caledonia Road.' On any other day we might have been wary of a Russian stranger pointing us towards our bed for the night, but to be perfectly honest with you, I never batted an eyelid. 'Take us there,' I told him, and off we went to find this house he'd heard about. We had no choice – we had to blag ourselves somewhere to stay until some money came through.

As we walked up to this house, I groaned. It was an old three-storey place, rammed with people, falling to pieces, no hot water, the front door half-hanging off and broken archway windows in the front door with dirty curtains blowing out of the holes into the street. It was a complete wreck. It looked like a bad squat.

We knocked on the door. The hinges looked as if they were about to fall off, they were shaking so much. This bloke opened the door and started speaking Italian at us. We asked, 'Room?' and he took us into this sitting room that had two beds and a couch stuffed into it. Then we met the woman who ran this wreck of a house, an old Italian woman called Maya. We admitted we had no jobs and it might be a while before we could pay rent, but as soon as we could we would back-pay everything. She thought about it and said, 'OK,' but by now we'd actually looked around and I, for one, was having a change of heart.

I turned to my two mates and said, 'We can't stay here, it is *that* bad, we can't do it.' So we politely said 'no'. At that stage, we genuinely thought someone would give us somewhere better to live. We started to walk off down the road, but after about a hundred yards, I changed my mind again, stopped and said, 'Lads, it's a roof over our heads, let's go...'

We turned back and moved in there and then.

That first night I slept in the place I wrapped myself up

and pulled the blankets over my head, it was so vile. The second night we were there, my bed frame broke in the middle so for the first four weeks I slept in a bed shaped like a 'V'. Fortunately, I am the type of person who can feel at home anywhere. A lot of people need a sense of belonging to feel comfortable, but I don't have that at all. No matter where I am, no matter what's going on, it could be a box or on top of a mountain, when I am done for the day, I hang my cap up and that's me, fast asleep.

There were forty Italians living there that first day we turned up. We were allocated a room on the ground floor where three other people were already living as well. So that was six of us, each paying £50 a week (yes, even more than we'd paid for that B&B on our first night), sleeping in one sitting room. Some of us slept on couches, a couple on mattresses and one on the floor. After a short while, the other three moved out so it was me, Ken and Lar living together in the sitting room. It was cold, wet, draughty, inconvenient, dirty, antisocial and as good as derelict. And you know what? It was one of the best experiences of my entire life. I was as happy as a pig in shit, literally!

Having said that, at times it was insane. Still without work, after a few days we were reduced to about £20 each, so we bought a giant bag of pasta, put some sauce all over it and lived off that for about a week. Each night after looking for jobs we would come back in and dip into this increasingly crusty and stale bowl of pasta for a tiny portion each. It was minging! Until this point I had been massive but started to lose weight because I wasn't eating properly – I am one of those people who has to train otherwise I lose weight. In four weeks I lost twenty-one pounds.

Pretty quickly, I came down to my last £10. I was desperate. We were starving and I must admit, I thought there was no hope, but I just couldn't bear the thought of having to go home to Ireland so soon. So I walked to the Tube station, handed over £5 for a one-day Travelcard and set off to the West End looking for work, a solitary fiver and some loose change in my pocket. I walked miles asking for a job, any job. Bars, clubs, shops, anything, places like Gap in Oxford Street, but no one would give me a job. It was incredibly demoralising but something inside me was saying *I am not leaving this country until I have done something!* Even though I was really down, I remember walking through Leicester Square and Piccadilly and all over the West End thinking, *Jesus! London is amazing!*

Since 8am I had been treading the pavements of the West End and by 3pm I was exhausted. I found myself in Trafalgar Square and sat down by the fountains. It was the very first time I had ever seen the Square and although it looked amazing, I was in no mood to be a tourist. I was dismayed: I had £5 in my pocket and still no job. No one was helping. I sat there for what seemed like forever, thinking to myself, *Something has always happened to make things work out, but is it going to this time?*

Then I overheard a few Irish accents and noticed a

group of lads sitting just across the way from me. We got talking, as you do, and they were asking me what was happening with me.

'I'm having an absolute nightmare, to be honest – I need a job.'

'Have you tried the sites?' one of them suggested.

'Sites? What do you mean?'

'The sites... building sites,' he replied. 'There's loads of 'em. We're working at this one in Earl's Court. Why don't you get down there and ask for this fella.' They gave me the name of the site manager and went on their way.

Using my Travelcard I got down there as quickly as I could, knowing that most sites close down around 4pm. I walked into this gaff, found the site manager and told the guy my story. Fortunately, this particular crew was working late on the site to catch up.

'Have you got any work for me?' I asked, as politely as I could.

'That depends, really, on what you work like. You see those plasterboards there? See how many of those you can get up to the top of the stairs before the end of the day.'

He didn't need to ask twice. I was massive at the time so I ran over and started taking three or four boards in one go. I was ripped to shit, wearing a yellow hard hat, a vest and my baggy shorts and all the other blokes on the site were singing, 'YMCA' at me, but I didn't care. Every single plasterboard in the pile went up there in about two hours. I did more work shifting them than his three labourers had done the whole of the day before. So he didn't care either.

When I reported back to him, he put sixty quid in my hand and said, 'Go home and come back Monday morning.'

I was nearly crying, I was so relieved.

'Mate, I can't tell you... you just saved me!'

'You fucking earned it!' he told me.

So I went home, ran into our room to find the lads and I've gone, 'Sixty pounds! Sixty fucking pounds!', waving it in the air like a trophy. It felt like a million pounds. We hadn't been eating properly for a few days so I took us all out for a slap-up meal at McDonald's. This is no word of a joke, but when I bit into this Big Mac, I swear to God it tasted like lobster, there was actually saliva coming out of my mouth and down my chin. We looked at each other eating these burgers and the feeling of pure happiness was just immense. We had got money; we were in with a chance. We were staying in London.

One day, shortly after I started the site job, I'd just got paid and was waiting on a platform for my train back home. We were still only just getting straight, starving, tired but glad to finally have some cash coming in. So I was standing there on this deserted platform in my site clothes, filthy dirty, my hard hat strapped to the side of my waist and my tool bag slung over my shoulder. Then I noticed out of the corner of my eye these two blokes walking in my direction and I could sense straight away there was going to be a situation. I thought to myself, *Oh my God, I can't believe this – we need this money!*

Then one of the guys pulled a knife out.

Problem was, he'd picked on a starving hungry, tired, desperate Irishman who'd just had a long, hard slog on a building site for his money. I'd have fucking died before I handed this cash over. Before they had chance to threaten me I said, 'Mate, I have got a fucking hammer in this bag here, if I have to get this hammer out I am going to batter you all!' I was so angry that the veins in my neck were bulging out and I was livid at the possibility they'd take our cash.

They looked at me and you could see the thought passing through their brains: *Shit, we've picked on a mentaller!*

They ran off.

The building site work lasted for about eight weeks, which perfectly bridged the gap until I got my security badge. I also signed on at an agency that used to give me random temp jobs. You had to get to their office at six-thirty in the morning and they would allocate your day's work to you. It sounds hard, but I was in my element. I was travelling round London, surviving, meeting new people, doing shit I had never done before. I was having a total ball. I loved meeting people, although the jobs were pretty mind numbing. One time I spent two weeks in Greenwich picking two-litre bottles of cola off the floor, wrapping them in plastic and putting them in boxes. Mind you, it was worth it to go on the DLR, my first time – coming from Ireland you've never really seen a transport system like that. I felt like Arnold Schwarzenegger in *Total Recall*.

When I think of that time now, it was mental, the shit we went through. The place where we lived really was a dump. We didn't have a door on our room at all and as we were by the front door, it was not very private. All the showers were broken and one side of the house so badly subsided we used to bet on when it would actually fall down. Eventually I got tired of having no door to our room, so I brought a plank of wood home from the building site and used that instead. When we went to sleep at nights, I just picked up the wood and placed it by the door frame. You could still stick your head in through a gap, but it was an improvement. My digs were shocking, I wasn't getting paid much money and the site was very hard work, but I was surviving: I was still in England and I didn't have to go home.

We'd complained about the lack of a proper door for weeks, but the Italian landlady didn't do anything about it. One night she walked in to ask for the rent money, going 'Darlings, darlings, I needa my money, please, I needa.' I was lying in the bed, looking up at this crazy character speaking to me when I noticed the door – which was precariously propped up on one side – begin to fall towards her. In slow motion, it fell on her head and she crashed on my bed, trapped underneath the door. So now she's on my bed with this plank on her, shouting 'Darlings, darlings, save me! Save me!' We got her out and she was OK, but I have to admit I nearly pissed myself laughing at the irony of the situation.

The site work really helped, but the main aim was to get that security badge as quickly as possible. We'd found out that the borough of Croydon was supposed to be the fastest at issuing them, so myself and Lar headed down there one day with all our paperwork to get ourselves licensed. We queued all day in the council offices, hours on end it was, but just as we stood beside each other at the counter for our turn, I got a chill on my neck, turned to Lar and said, 'Nah! I am going to Westminster to get my badge! Don't do it! Come with me to Westminster!'

'You what, Fran?' asked Lar.

'Come with me to Westminster. Trust me, I don't know why, I've just got a feeling, come on!'

He thought I was mad, not least because we'd spent all day queuing and were about to hand in our papers for a badge. He said 'no' and gave his papers over the counter.

I actually ran out of the Croydon Council offices, got on the Tube and went straight to Westminster. To this day, I don't know why I did it, I just got a feeling that Croydon was not right and Westminster was. So I went with that feeling. I came up the stairs out of Westminster Tube and stood there looking at Big Ben, amazed. I'd never seen it before. I asked someone where the council building was and found my way to the relevant office.

Once there I queued again, then handed in my papers for my badge.

All the time I was waiting for my badge, I was training hard in the gym and working like a dog on the building site, so by the time the badge came through I was massive. Ironically, despite what everyone had told us about Croydon, I got my badge two weeks before Lar. And he was working in a borough he didn't want to be in. As soon as I got my badge in my hand, I walked up to the front door of the superclub Home in Leicester Square, which had only recently opened, looking for work.

Within two weeks, I was head doorman.

# CHAPTER EIGHT

# HOME LIFE

Home had opened with a big fanfare as supposedly the first of a generation of new 'superclubs'. It was an enormous multi-storeyed building in Leicester Square, one of the most expensive sites in the whole of Europe – and probably the world. No expense had been spared on its ultra-lavish interior. Paul Oakenfold was the resident DJ – he came down from Cream and some other guys joined him in what was effectively almost a World XI of big-name DJs. The total cost of setting Home up was rumoured to be around the £10 million mark.

The story of how I got a job there is typical of so many things I have done. I had my doorman's badge in my pocket, fresh from being stamped just down the road in Westminster Council offices. The first night I got my badge, I got off the building site bang on time, went to the gym, then went home and changed into my black doorman's gear, then headed into Leicester Square. Once I got there, I literally stood at the front door of

Home asking for a job. The doormen were like, 'Yeah, whatever!'

I stood there for two hours and kept asking.

Later in the evening, I could see a lady behind them who, it transpired, was the manager of the club. I was still banging on about wanting to work there and I could see she was listening, so I spoke louder and more animatedly to get her attention. Eventually, she walked over and said, 'Look, come back into the office next week and I'll give you an interview.' I thanked her for her time and left.

The very next day, I left the site bang on time again, went to the gym, went home and got changed into my black gear and headed into Leicester Square once more. This time I managed to blag my way past the front door and worked my way up all the stairs until I got to the manager's office. I knocked.

'Come in.'

'Hello again, you said to come in to see you for an interview, so here I am!'

'No, I said come in next week for an interview – I can't do it right now,' she said, with a frown rippling across her brow.

'Oh, I'm really sorry, I thought you said today...' I knew I was pushing my luck. 'Well, look, I'm here now, you may as well have a chat...'

'I can't, why don't you come back...'

Just then the phone rang.

I swear to God, no word of a lie, it was a regular doorman phoning in sick.

She finished up the call and looked at me and asked, 'When can you start?'

I fluffed up my lapels on my suit and said, 'How about now?'

They sent me from the office straight to Level 4 of Home to start work that very night. I'd only had my badge forty-eight hours: I was on my way, I just knew it. Two weeks later I was head doorman. How? It was simple. Luckily for me, just after I joined the security company in charge changed and loads of personnel moved on. I was there at the right time and in the right place and I wasn't about to let that opportunity pass me by. One opportunity to prove myself came when we opened the entire club – 1,700 punters and thousands of square feet of space – with just six doorman on duty... and we pulled it off. If I'd been working at Croydon, I would have still been waiting for my badge. Instead, I was head of security at the biggest superclub in Europe.

Home quickly became famous among clubbers, although not always for the right reasons. From the start it was riddled with problems – in fact, in my opinion, the whole thing was a disaster. In a sense, Leicester Square was the worst site for a superclub because real clubbers would be confronted by thousands of tourists and messiness, and scumbags and fights all over the streets. It was just not a good mix.

Having said all that, I learned so much from working at Home. The company who ran the club made this big deal about how you could progress up the ranks from within, how they would open up opportunities and so on. Looking back now, that was a crock of shit, but at the time it inspired me to help myself get on. Back then, I was just a doorman, but the whole time I was there I was striving to get myself off the door and promoted some way, regardless of whether the company helped me or not.

To be fair, while I worked there, Home was my life. I used to go in at three or four in the afternoon ready for work that night. One of my best jobs at Home was being what is called a 'picker'. I had to keep my eye out for people we didn't want in the club. Although everyone else used to wear regulation black suits, I often wore baggy trousers and a white T-shirt, keeping things really cool. One night the manager gave me this spiel about dressing correctly, but I did my own thing. Some of the pickers would stand and talk with the queue, trying to figure out who was coming in or not, but when I was on the door, I would always argue with them – they took far too long. I knew instantaneously, 'Yes, no, yes, no, yes, no, keep them moving!' I used to be stepping in all the time so eventually I was made a picker myself.

Door Nazis, pickers, there are loads of names for them. It goes on at a lot of clubs – it's pure elitism. At my first big pick, I met this guy called Paratosh. He came strolling down the stairs with a baby blue jacket on, skiing glasses, a mad cap and a big cigar hanging out of his mouth. I said to a doorman, 'What a cool-looking bastard. Who's he?'

They replied, 'It's Paratosh, the head picker, Paul Oakenfold chose him personally.' The first time I met him he was definitely giving it the 'You're just a doorman' vibe, but over time we became friends and ended up working at other clubs together later on. Nice bloke, I liked him.

One of the best ways of avoiding trouble in any club is not to allow suspicious-looking people in there in the first place. More often than not they were lads who'd had far too much to drink already. So it was my job to go up to these groups of lads and tell them they were not coming in.

I used to go out into Leicester Square by myself and there would be two or three hundred people in the queue, winding around the streets. Even though there'd be ten doormen at front of house, I would always do this work on my own – I didn't need anyone else to sort it out. It was like my own private show. I would go up to a particular group of lads who couldn't be allowed in, give them a firm but friendly handshake, apologise and say, 'You're not going to be able to come in tonight, lads...' and speak to them with a smile and respect. I only ever got into one scrap out there in the Square because every time I refused someone, they'd shake my hand and say, 'At least you're a decent bloke and have spoken to us like normal people and with respect.' It was all about how I talked to people. Of course, I knew I could walk the walk too and that sense of self-confidence if it comes to a scrap must have pervaded my chat.

People were lovely to me, even when I was refusing

them. After I got to England, and specifically when I was working at Home, I couldn't believe the reception I got from people, from girls, from blokes; people really loved the Irish personality. And I'd never had so much attention from girls in my life. I had a brilliant time out there.

Not wishing to sound cocky, but I think it's fair to say I was a good doorman. To get that position at Home speaks for itself, I guess, but I do think I was good at my job. The reasons I excelled as a doorman were various: I viewed every punter with humility and respect, I never let my ego interfere with a confrontation, I understood situations very quickly and could read people before they had even spoken a word, I could sense an atmosphere – almost to the point where I knew it was going to kick off a while before it actually did – and I was able to handle the situation if it did get out of hand. People pay a lot of money for 'life-coaching' classes, but if you want a crash course in understanding people, go and work the doors at a nightclub.

Working on the door is acting. Before each shift I would put on my shoes and suit, and walk in there almost as an alter ego of myself. I did not bring in my pride, that was for the other person to do – it's not about my ego. I didn't get insulted by people or by situations: I was able to leave the negative things to one side... I have been asked about acting work and I would love to have a go, although I would be starting something completely new. But I do think that because of my door work, I have been acting in one form or another since I was 17. As a quick aside, around this time I had a screen test for a part in a movie that a mate of mine was involved with – the role was that of a gypsy boxer! They had this car and I was supposed to sit on top of it and look hard, but I thought that sounded pretty lame. Instead, I ran up and jumped on the roof and started smashing this car to pieces, took the windscreen out, everything! The look on their faces was priceless – they loved it. I didn't get the part, though!

Getting back to door work, I don't like to dwell on the fighting aspect of that job, but sometimes people ask what it's like to go to work knowing you might end up having a scrap. It's weird, but it never bothered me. I get scared too, I'll be honest with you, especially on the occasions when you know you only just got out of a situation. However, that fear rarely, if ever, intrudes on my work. When it does kick off, I go into this strange mode where I am blinkered to everything except the confrontation that is erupting. I don't see people, I see situations, and I think that has helped me stay relatively fresh-faced. Heading towards the age of 30 and having worked doors for well over a decade, I don't have any scars on my face. I've had a few bad bangs but touch wood I've been quite lucky. I have been in a lot of scraps and getting this far without a scar is, in all fairness, quite an achievement.

Another reason I am not as scarred as many of my friends is because I avoid more fights. I don't want to sound overly spiritual here, but I do believe in energies in people. I think different people exude different energies and I have learned to make the most of this when I work on the doors. I have walked through the West End of London with a Selfridges bag full of £20,000 in cash but not once worried about being mugged. I am convinced that if you give off an air of self-assured confidence, certain things are less likely to happen to you. Having grown from a kid who was probably exuding all the wrong energies and possibly even attracting bad situations, I know the opposite is also true. If someone had approached me when I was carrying that bag, they would have felt something and decided against it.

I have spent my whole life watching, analysing, trying to understand, reading body language, the way people sit, they way they talk, the tone of their voice, and I have made myself an expert in that. This is why nine times out of ten when a situation arises on the door I am able to avoid using physical solutions. I can have a bloody good scrap but I will always first look someone straight in the eyes and most people pick up on that and go 'Nah, better not.'

After a while, I started running the VIP section of Home. Friday nights was fantastic: me, their cool door picker on the VIP door, with hundreds of people outside literally *begging* to get in. I was always dressed cool and met loads of deadly people. The door itself was on the side of the club and the VIP room was on the sixth floor. It was a really good bar and always rammed with celebrities. To be honest, working the VIP room brings you into contact with a different class of punter than working than the front door, where it can all get a bit lairy. You worked the VIP door by yourself because they needed more men for the front of house.

I met so many interesting people working that VIP door. Obviously lots of celebs used to go there, but there were also people like lawyers, accountants and of course, newspaper journalists. One of the most famous journalists is Rav from *News of the World* and I first met him there in 1999 when he was working for *The Sun*. He walked up to the VIP room at Home with a few people like Dom Mohan and all that. I had seen pictures of him but never in person, so it was interesting to meet him. Rav used to come to Home all the time for meetings and to look after people, so I got to know him very well from the door. Eventually we became friends and I still really like Rav, we get on really well. Always a gentleman and at the top of his game too.

Everyone went there, it was really cool. I was always down on the door but the parties they had were wild. One night there'd been some big television awards and afterwards loads of soap stars were out on the town in the West End. I'd met Sid Owen – who played Ricky Butcher – a few times and he came down to the door with a few other cast members, so I said hi and led them upstairs past the queue. About fifteen minutes later some more cast members came up to me, and I thought, *Oh, OK, I can just about squeeze these in too*. I took them up and walked back down the stairs and when I got to the door, what seemed like the entire cast of *EastEnders* was standing there! It turned out Sid had phoned round people and said the party was at Home. The problem was, the management were really weird about things like that – it wasn't a given that everyone could come in. For me, I would have let them in, they were all famous soap stars and that can only be good for a club. But Home wasn't that straightforward. Tamzin Outhwaite was there with her bloke, Ian Beale, all of them, it was bizarre. I knew I would get in trouble but I let them all in too.

Then I get a call on the radio from the owner of the club and he asks, 'What the fuck is going on in my VIP room, Fran? It's like a fucking episode of *EastEnders* in here! Stop the door!' He came down and grabbed me, 'What's going on?' He proper grilled me, he really did! It was a surreal night.

At the end of each night, one of the security team would stand on the door to let people know the club was closed. The door itself was about ten feet wide, but by that stage of the night you could look after it yourself. One night I was standing there when I saw these six huge, black guys coming across Leicester Square, obviously heading towards Home. I was like, Oh great!

They got right up to me and five of these guys were absolutely massive. However, they were standing around this smaller guy – I say smaller, he was still nearly six foot and absolutely solid. I'm looking at this guy, who had his head bowed and then he turned his face up to mine... and it was Mike Tyson.

Bollocks!

'I'd like to come in the club with my friends here,' he said, politely.

I was trying to stay calm, but I was already thinking, this is not a good situation. Don't get me wrong, I can handle myself and have always been a good scrapper – but Mike Tyson...

'I'm really sorry, gents, the club is closed and I can't let you in, I'm afraid.'

'But we want to come in,' he said, again politely.

I was effectively in a standoff with one of the greatest heavyweight boxers in history and five of his mates. I've been in better situations.

'Look,' I said as calmly as I could, 'if you try to come in I will have to try to stop you, and don't get me wrong I will give it a good shot, but then you will batter me and then we will have a problem. Plus we will all get sacked, every man in here.'

Tyson looked me straight in the eye for a second.

That second felt like an hour. The buzz and noise and commotion of Leicester Square fell silent in my mind and all I could see was Tyson, one of the most famous men in the world, this massive powerful neck and his eyes looking at me. Silence. I even felt my body tense in readiness for what would undoubtedly be the hardest punch I had ever taken.

Then he held out his hand to shake mine and said, 'You are a gentleman, thank you for speaking with us like that, I will leave you in peace.' And with that, Tyson calmly walked away into the night.

I'd like to say I handled it all as calm as you like, but to be honest, I'd pure shit myself! As me da used to say to me, the sun shines down on a dog's backside at least once in its life and that was my turn.

Mind you, famous people can often get out of hand too. One time I had a situation with two professional rugby players. I was inside and I heard a massive ruckus at the door, so I ran to find these rugby players pushing these two girls around. I looked at them and they were giants – I was big at the time, but these two were monsters. I walked straight over and said, 'Lads, what's the story here?' and they growled something at me that sounded like, 'Gggrrrrr!'

I looked at these two blokes and I knew instantly I was not going to win any scrap. They were too big, they were out there pissed and already aggressive. If you were lucky, you might down one of them, but not both and they'd probably get straight back up – after all, they were rugby players and therefore used to being flattened all the time. They were growling some more and moving towards me – I knew I needed a different approach, and fast.

'Hey mate,' I said to the biggest one of the two. 'Just look up there, that's a brand-new video camera, look, just been fitted and you are on TV at the moment, a bit like *Candid Camera*, only this time you are the star. Listen, you feel free to come over and start battering me, I'll give you that. But I will make one radio call and twenty doormen will come round here and batter you – so everyone is going to get battered. But I tell you what is also going to happen: that video tape is going to be sitting in a tabloid newspaper's office come Monday morning with you two – professional rugby players – attacking a doorman in the street and that's going to be all over the front page. Mate, you are going to get a bollocking off your manager, which is no good to anyone, is it?'

They looked at me, their massive chests heaving with adrenalin and then, suddenly, the biggest one started laughing. He slapped me on the shoulder with this bucket-like hand and said, 'You are a mad bastard. Very nice to meet you,' and then quietly left.

Just after my friend Rachel came in to do the VIP door with me, they moved me back to the street-side because it had been getting really messy out front. One night a fight had started and a doorman radioed me and said, 'Fran, there's a guy in the lift, there's a pregnant woman in there too, he won't get out and everyone is freaking out.' They used to have girls in the lift, you see, to escort people to various floors, so immediately this sounded very tricky. So I went up to try to persuade this guy to come out quietly but he was having none of it. Then he went for me so I wrapped him in a headlock. As soon as I did that, this pregnant woman jumped on my back and started punching me in the head. Somehow I managed to drag him out under one arm while carefully carrying the woman on my back into the street. At least they were out of the lifts and out of the club now, I thought. But my troubles were not over.

The woman would just not stop hitting me, so I very carefully placed her down on the ground, but as I did so her boyfriend came running up to kick me in the head. At the same time, three of his mates started piling in too, so then it all went off with them and all the doormen began this fight on the street. But do you know what happened? No one got badly hit and I orchestrated our team and got everyone off the street to retreat back into Home.

When we were almost back inside, one of these drunken blokes found a bag of bottles and stated hurling them at us. I saw one come in fast and managed to flick my head out of the way but the broken bottle just smashed into the arm of a doorman behind me. He ended up with eighteen stitches in his arm (the glass ripped right down the back of his tricep) and he was out of work for three months.

But still the original troublemaker wasn't happy. We were trying to close the door, but the bloke who'd refused to leave the lift got hold of the steel barriers that rope the queues in and started swinging it wildly around. I decided to let him blow himself out – after all, no one was getting hurt, he was breaking a few of the club's windows but there no lasting damage was being done and it stopped the fight spilling back out on to the streets. We were under strict orders not to fight with punters or be seen physically beating the shit out of people in the Square because the company running Home said that was not the right image at all. So the whole time I reacted to this aggression by trying to do what was best for the club.

Eventually, the guy got tired and ran off. Then one of the managers of the club came out and asked, 'What happened? Why didn't you beat the shit out of him?' I was like, 'Mate, make up your mind! You wanted a safe environment and a controlled security system, a window got smashed but it's better than going out in the street and beating the shit out of someone, isn't it?' I was so frustrated. That was one of the first times I started to wonder how much longer I wanted to work at Home.

There were some truly bizarre incidents at the club too. One night Carl Cox and Danny Agnew were playing to a sell-out crowd. At the time the club was being refurbished – in this room, for example, they had moved the DJ booth around – so there was a hole in the roof above the DJ box. As Danny was playing, water started pouring down through the ceiling onto his head! I got a call on the radio saying, 'Danny's had to stop playing,' but by the time I got there, Carl Cox had started his set. And the solution? They just stood behind him with an umbrella!

On a positive note, one of the most amazing things about Home was the view of London from the roof. Everywhere I have ever gone I've always had a base, somewhere in town. In London it's always been in the West End, somewhere that was mine or somewhere I worked. The building that housed Home was like that to me.

So many of the Home crew were like family: Lar had come over as assistant head doorman for me and I became close friends with loads of others. We had some great nights out, but also shared one particularly relaxing routine. On a Sunday morning, myself and most of the doormen used to climb up to the very top of the building, thirteen floors up, climb outside on to the roof itself, then up this massive ladder onto the top platform. From there you could see every part of London, every single part. I used to sit on the side of the building with my feet dangling down over the edge, in the sunshine with a beer and my mates, thinking *Yes! London!* That building is still my favourite one in England because it's where I started off, it's where I hang around in town to this day, and I will always come back to it. When I was young, London was always the best place with the coolest clubs and there I was, perched on the top of the biggest superclub, sipping a beer with my mates. It was a fantastic feeling.

One great memory of Home is of when my little brother Adam came over to London as a young teenager and I took him to the club. He got in all the best rooms, I took a photograph of him holding the guest list and he stood on the door with me. I also showed him all around the West End too – it was wicked.

I made some life-long friends during my time at Home. One night I was standing outside at three in the morning when I met this bird, who started talking to me and eventually invited me to a party. I normally don't need to be asked twice so we headed off to this small club called Pop in Golden Square. I knocked on the door and this black guy peered through the door and asked, 'Who are you?' 'My name's Fran, I am the head doorman at Home,' I told him, 'Who are you?' 'Isaac,' he replied, shook my hand and let us in.

We went down to the club and there were only about ten people in there after closing time having late drinks, with this other black guy on the decks playing some wicked tunes. We walked in the back room and Isaac turned to me and asked, 'Do you drink whisky?' 'I sure as hell do!' I replied. He left the room and then came back with a really expensive bottle of bourbon, stuck it on the table with two glasses and sat down next to me. Bear in mind, this was the first time I'd ever met him.

It was about 3.30am. By noon the next day we'd only just finished drinking and when we crawled out of Pop onto Oxford Street, we were both absolutely bolloxed. It was a wicked night. That night I also met a fantastic bloke called Dave, who used to DJ at Pop too. Unfortunately Dave has been struck down with a serious illness, which was devastating news, as we have been best mates forever, man. He's a legend, he really is.

A big group of us used to hang out there all the time. We were one of the tightest crews in London – everywhere you went everyone knew you and everyone else seemed to want to know you; a proper gang it was. Proper handshakes too, just deadly, the best ever! I remember a few times I'd be out with all these friends pinching myself and thinking I was so lucky. Every single night was the best night of my life.

My time at Home was running out, though. The club

was too big, the confusion and the movement around the building dire. People used to queue to get in, then queue to get into a dance room, then queue to get into the toilet, queue again to get back into the dance room! It was shit for clubbers, brutal. As I said, though, I loved it for a long time – I even worked on the eve of the new Millennium.

I always wanted to be more than a doorman and at first the company behind Home made me feel like that was possible with them. It gradually became apparent, however, that this was not actually the case and I started to get disillusioned. Once I begin to lose heart in something, I find it difficult to sustain interest. On more than one occasion I ended up having massive run-ins with the management: I just felt they had changed the parameters of what they wanted and it wasn't a situation I felt I could work with any more. Eventually, I had a meeting with the same female manager who had given me the job in the first place. I told her, 'This is bullshit, I am not staying because I am not progressing any more, and I thought that was encouraged.' It had reached the point where I had done everything I felt I could do and was gradually disagreeing with the management at the club more and more. One night I felt I just couldn't be involved with what was going on any more, so even though I was head doorman, I quit.

'I'll finish my night's work, of course,' I told them, but they said I was to leave immediately and closed the door.

# CHAPTER NINE

# MOVING ON AGAIN

I lived at the house in Caledonia Road for almost twelve months. My working life at Home might have introduced me to some of the country's biggest celebrities, but my own 'home' life was altogether more down-to-earth. Back at the near squat, we were now sharing our digs with a Chinese guy called Yoshi, who lived in the kitchen press.

We had been used to conditions being pretty squalid but were still surprised one morning when a wrinkly old Chinese man walked into our bedroom unannounced.

'Sorry, mate, but who are you?'

'I am Yoshi,' he said.

'OK, nice to meet you, what's your story, then?'

It turns out that Maya had known Yoshi and his wife for a while and we gradually found out about his life. His wife had passed away and, because he was an illegal, her family took all their property away from him and kicked him out onto the streets. He was an illegal, so could do absolutely nothing about it. At first Yoshi was living in the back room of the house but as it became more and more crowded, he moved and ended up living in the kitchen press.

We all used to give him a pound a week, for which he used to clean the kitchen, wash the dishes and all that. I used to give him more money, buy him drinks and let him eat my food. One night we were in having a few drinks – it was such a stark contrast to life in Dublin, because over there we'd been working the doors, we'd be out every night, earning good money and enjoying ourselves. In London for that first year, we just couldn't afford to go out at all. We had the usual five channels on the old television and nothing to entertain ourselves but a few cans.

After several of these cans had been drunk and we were all getting into bed, I went out to the toilet. I could see that Yoshi was pissed out of his face – he was standing there in the room, this mad old Chinese man, a wrinkly creature hunched over in grubby red Y-fronts. He looked like an older and drunker version of Gollum from *The Lord of the Rings*.

I went to the toilet then walked back in to our room to find Yoshi standing over the bed where Ken was asleep, chanting in this weird whisper, 'Ah, so this is the higher power!' Ken was dead to the world, so he didn't know this was going on.

'What the fuck are you doing, Yoshi?' I asked, struggling to keep myself from laughing. Yoshi just looked at me in a daze, turned to Ken's bed, lifted the blanket and got into bed with him.

I was pissing myself laughing, thinking *Should I wake Ken up? What should I do?* I snuck over to where Lar was sleeping and said, 'Lar, Yoshi is in Ken's bed!' Lar rubbed his eyes and looked around, then started pissing himself laughing too.

At this point, Yoshi grumbled something and put his arm around Ken. I had to say something so I went over to the bed and said, 'Ken!'

'What?' he asked, squinting from tiredness.

'Your boyfriend is in bed with you!'

Ken jumped so high I swear he nearly hit the ceiling. He leapt out of bed and yelled at Yoshi, 'What the fuck are you doing?' It was absolutely hilarious. I was aching from laughing.

The kitchen press where Yoshi lived was only a few feet square. I got hold of an old mattress for him so at least he had something to sleep on. But when I came to put it in, it was too big and wouldn't fit – that's how small the press was. So I got hold of the mattress, placed it up against the entrance hole, walked across to the other side of the room and then came running back across and jumped into this bed like a bulldozer... There was a loud snapping sound and when we looked up, the mattress had somehow fitted in. Yoshi lived there for six months.

We were constantly playing practical jokes on each other. There were rats all over the place and they were always scurrying around in the room. I got hold of a cricket bat to take to bed at night because you could hear all the mice and rats running round under the boards. When I heard them, I would just smack the cricket bat on the floor. If I managed to catch hold of one of them, they would go flying across the room and hit the walls.

Lar was a tough nut, but I set him up proper one night. We were all in bed and he was dozing off. As I put my feet by the side of my bed, I noticed the floorboard between us was broken. If I pushed my foot down, the board on the other side of the room by Lar was going up. I waited until I could hear him asleep, then put his shoes on top of this floorboard by his bed. Then, at the top of my voice, I shouted 'Lar! Lar! There's a rat in your shoe!'

Lar yelped out loud and jumped up then leant over his shoe in the dark. As he did so, I pushed my foot down hard and the floorboard leapt up at him. He jumped a mile and totally shit himself. Some tough nut!

Another night, I stuck a piece of fish-wire under Ken's plate. The idea was that every time Lar said something and Ken looked at him, I would tug this wire and pull his plate further and further away from him. So Lar said something to catch his attention and I yanked the wire. Instead of moving an inch or two, the whole plate of steaming hot food crashed all over Ken and onto the floor. Ken went mad! The next morning, I was lying under my blanket fast asleep when Ken caught hold of my bed and toppled me off onto the floor. I was swearing and shouting after him, but he ran out, leaving the front door open. As he ran past our broken front window, I could hear him laughing to himself all the way down the street.

At first there were all those Italians in the house but then a load of Paddies moved in. We were physically massive and I think our 'house mates' thought of us as three Irish psychopaths in the front room. There was a New Zealand and Aussie couple we got along with great too; basically, we were all just working to survive and trying to get on. Lar hated the Italians and they hated him but apart from that it was great at first. After several months, however, a load of dickheads moved in, who were playing their music too loud all night long (and for me to say that, you know that must have been loud!), so the other two lads started talking about moving out and getting our own apartment together. We'd got a bit of money together – I'd been working at Home for months by now – so we started looking at flats to rent and found a place that looked pretty decent.

Then, for some reason, just before we were due to move out, I got that familiar feeling again.

'I can't do it, lads. I don't know why, but I want to stay on here.'

So I did.

The other two lads were not best pleased with me, to be honest. One of us would have had a very small bedroom, but that wasn't especially why I changed my mind. Like the coin flip, the Croydon badge counter and now this, I just had a sense it wasn't the right thing to do.

It turned out to be another of the best decisions I ever made.

It was a shame that it caused friction between the three of us after we'd had such good times in the house, though. I was stressed about the whole move so I said I would work the night they were due to leave. When I came back the next morning I found a ton of wallpaper pulled off and on the floor in my room. Clearly, they were really pissed off with me for pulling out. They eventually got a nice gaff together and we just went our separate ways.

This wasn't the only big change I made in my life at this time. Just two weeks later I quit my job at Home. I went home that night and sat down, with part of me thinking, *What are you doing?* Within the space of a few days, I had gone from lodging with two good mates and having a laugh, as well as being head of security at one of Europe's highest-profile nightclubs, to being on my own in a squat with no job. And do you know what? It felt absolutely right.

I actually found I enjoyed my own company for a while: I took the time away from work to train really hard every day, sometimes twice a day and I got into fantastic shape and ate, slept and drank training for about five weeks or so. I'd already been massive when I was working at Home so by the end of this intensive training spell, I was absolutely huge.

I decided to go back to Ireland to visit my family and friends. I was shaven-headed, eighteen stone and packed with muscle. My arms alone were eighteen inches around the biceps. I came through Arrivals and my dad walked straight past me: he didn't even recognise me.

I had a great couple of weeks in Ireland catching up with old friends – I'd told all the doormen in Dublin that I'd got really skinny, so when this hulking bloke walked up to them they were like, 'Aaahh! Fran! Look at you!' They were all really pleased for me – 'We hear you're doing really well for yourself, fair play to you, Fran.' That was really nice and respect to them for that. Unfortunately, it wasn't all plain sailing. I also made an almighty embarrassment of myself with me ma. I'd been working so hard in London that I really wanted to blow off some steam and reassess. I have to admit I was a bit wild at that point and one night I got really pissed and took a woman back to me ma's gaff. That might seem harmless enough, of course, but what we chose to do when we got there wasn't. I was shagging her over the kitchen table when me ma walked in!

This was one of the most embarrassing moments in my entire life; I was mortified. It was such an open disrespect of me ma and her house. Ma just walked out in silence. I waited a while then stumbled up to bed but because I was so pissed I forgot I wasn't in my London digs and went to the wrong door, waltzing stark-bollock naked into my parents' bedroom. Aaahhh!

This was the first time I had been back from London so it was just awful – my parents must have wondered what I had turned into. I wasn't usually like that, of course, I was just letting my hair down after a long stretch of working incredibly hard. The next day I got out of bed and me da took me to one side and asked, 'What on earth did you do last night?' Then, as if the embarrassment wasn't already enough, he said, 'Come and have a look at this,' and he picked a blonde hair off the kitchen table. 'You've really upset your ma, you idiot.'

After my fortnight in Dublin, I flew back to London to decide on my next plan of action. I was out for a few drinks with my mates in Leicester Square when this guy walked past us and said, 'Fran, I've been trying to contact you, there's a brand-new VIP nightclub opening and I want you to run it.' All I was doing at the time was standing outside a bar, having a drink. That's what I mean about something always seems to come along for me.

I went in for a meeting and met everyone involved and they gave me the job as head of security at Red Cube, which was a massive celebrity club at the time. By now, I was well known on the club circuit and knew a lot of faces about town, so people started to come down to the club from all over the place. Mind you, if I was getting any ideas above my station, there were always people there to remind me of my roots! One night I was out with a load of people at Pop, after Red Cube had closed down for the evening. I walked in and who should be sitting there but

Jackie, the wife of security man Paul Higgins (who would shortly play a major part in my next phase of life). Now bear in mind that I was the host of this ultra-cool club with celebrities dripping off the walls. I could get into any VIP room in town, my entire reputation was built around being super-cool, big, and able to handle myself either in a fight or in a business meeting.

Jackie saw me and said, 'You're the little skinny bloke from the video shop!'

My doormen mates were in stitches. She was so funny; she always just used to abuse me. Jackie is a wickedly funny woman and she held court that night. She sat at one of the tables like an Indian princess, circled by all these enormous men listening to her every word. She told them loads of stories about me from when I was just a kid – I never lived it down!

It's actually not just the fights or drunken punters at clubs that can provide the most testing situations. One time I was working as head of security in a certain London nightclub when there was a meeting of two 'families' in the upstairs restaurant. We are talking large, very powerful families. During the course of this meeting, they spent a fortune on fine food, wine and champagne and the plan was to come down to the club below for the rest of the night. Just as they were finishing up at the table, the club's owner came over to me, clearly with something on his mind.

'Fran, they are not allowed in the club,' he said, gesturing with his head towards their table.

I couldn't believe my ears.

'Mate! Are you joking me? Do you know who they are?'

'Yes, and they are not coming in my club.'

All the doormen were looking at me as head of security and I was thinking *How the hell do I deal with this?* Obviously I was a little bit freaked out because this situation could go either way and if they chose to, these guys would just pound you down.

So I made my way over to their table.

'Sorry, can I sit down with you for a second?'

'Sure,' they said. 'What's up?'

I took a deep breath and said, 'Listen, sorry to interrupt you. There's a little bit of a problem...' As I began talking, I was scanning around the table to see who all the lads were looking to, because in a situation like that, people will always look to one person for direction. You can pick out the person everyone listens to pretty quickly and in this instance, I needed to.

I clocked him: a small guy sitting at the very end of the table. So I started talking to him, fixing my gaze straight in his eyes.

'Unfortunately, the owner of this venue doesn't want to allow you downstairs. Now, before you say anything, I am just one bloke sitting here among you guys and if you want to, you could throw me off the balcony right now and be done with it, but that's not what I am saying to you. At the end of the day, I make about six pounds an hour – I only do this job to feed myself. We've all got our individual personal issues but because I am the head of security here, if you go downstairs tonight, me and all my mates will lose our jobs.'

There was a pause. I felt like I was in a game of poker.

One of the men to the side started to say, 'Hold on a minute, we've spent a fortune in here...' but then the main man began to talk and the other guy instantly fell quiet.

'What would you like us to do?' he says.

This was a tough hand.

'I'd like you to not have this situation in the first place, *but* as we do, I'd like it if, when you have finished here, you would kindly go off to a different venue.' I kept talking. 'To be honest, not that you need my help, but loads of my friends run the clubs round here so if you want to go somewhere else, I can sort you out straight away.'

There was another slight pause and finally the main guy at the end of the table nodded his head slightly and said, 'Not a problem, not a problem.' Then he got them all to stand up there and then and walked them out of the venue. As we moved downstairs he turned to me and shook my hand then said, 'That is the most polite way that anyone has ever spoken to me in my whole life.'

I don't mind admitting I was pretty relieved to have thought on my feet and resolved what could have been a very difficult situation. So you can imagine my initial reaction when, fifteen minutes later, the main guy and one of his big friends came back into the club and walked straight over to me.

'What can I do for you, gentlemen?'

'Actually, we own a massive nightclub and were wondering if we can give you a job?' he said.

It was the closing hand.

'Thank you very much for that kind offer, gentlemen, and I'd like to say "yes" but I am responsible for all these guys here and if I leave, they won't have a job.' After I had politely declined, we shook hands again and they left.

To this day, I still see the main guy around quite often and whenever he sees me, he always says, 'If you have ever got any problems, you let me know...'

At the end of the day, the mere fact that I was respectful resolved that situation. People might look at people like me and think I can only fight, but being polite is one of the most powerful weapons in my armoury. It's also the decent way to live.

I like being around partying and people enjoying themselves; I actually strive to make people happy, it's one of my major goals in life, almost like some in-built instinct I can't deny or alter. I like to see people happy because I have felt unhappy plenty of times in my life, and it's not nice. I have felt the odd one out, the one with no mates, just wishing some days that someone would say something nice to me. So I will always be nice to people, whether it is through good manners or through my actions towards them. To be polite, humble and respectful is something everybody possesses inside them – it's not like you have to buy these skills. They can change your life; they certainly changed mine.

# CHAPTER TEN

# **TASH**

While I was working at Home, I would naturally see a lot of celebrities, bands, actors and other famous people. One of the groups down there quite often was Westlife. I didn't know them, although obviously I remember the first time I heard them on the radio. However, I was old friends with their security man, Paul Higgins, from Ireland (whose wife Jackie had called me 'the skinny guy' and told all those tales about me!). Paul was always telling me how busy he was looking after the band – who were absolutely massive at the time – and eventually he asked if I wanted to help out on a few shifts in the UK. I'd got to know the lads quite well by then, so I was really pleased to be asked. Then, after a few weeks of shift work for them, Paul said they were heading out on a major international tour in a couple of months and would I like to work for them full-time? I couldn't believe my luck. At this point, I was single and for a doorman to get a shot at anything to do with looking after celebrities and the chance to travel around the world with a massive band was the stuff of dreams. Maybe me da's *Bodyguard* jacket from all those years ago in the video shop had meant more than I realised at the time...

With the job I did for Westlife you never slept. It was comfortably one of the hardest jobs I've ever had in my whole life. You'd be up first thing in the morning to get one of the lads ready for interviews or whatever promotional work they were doing. You'd also be the last one to bed because you had to make sure they were in their rooms safely and sorted before you put your head down. Most days I was a walking ghost. Don't get me wrong: I'm not complaining about it – you know what the job entails when you take it on, so you just get on with it. We all worked very hard, the security and the band. What people don't realise is that a band like that works their bollocks off, all they do is solid graft. Of course, it's a good job and they make great money, but they do have to work their arses off.

The last thing you do when you are working as security for a pop band is to date another pop star. Paul Higgins had even said to me when I started, 'Don't fall for anyone in a band, Fran, OK?' So you can imagine the complications when I found myself falling in love with Natasha 'Tash' Hamilton of Atomic Kitten.

Tash had been out a few times around London and I had bumped into her or seen her about. Initially I thought she was a very good-looking girl, obviously, but I didn't fancy her. She is stunning, but at that point in my life I didn't look at her in the way that I do now. Besides, way back then, she was kind of seeing someone on and off. At this point I hadn't long been working with Westlife. The first inkling I had that something was going on was when I saw her out one night in Red Cube with her boyfriend and I felt really pissed off! I had barely spoken to her a few times then and I remember thinking to myself, *What is wrong with me? This is weird!*

Westlife were doing a Disney Awards in Home one time and the Kittens were there too, and I was set to look after the boys for the day. I kept finding myself looking at Tash – I just wasn't able to keep my eyes off her. One of the first times she came and spoke to me properly we were at a gig in Liverpool and she was with her tour manager. I could see she was looking at me but we were quite a distance apart; then the next thing I know, I looked round and she was sitting right beside me. Tash doesn't give a shit – if she wants something, she will go out there and get it! We had a laugh and chatted a little longer, joking about a Scouser I lived with and getting on really well straight away. But it was bizarre because I remember looking at Tash while she was chatting away and thinking, *Oh my God! I am gonna be with her, what is it about her?* We'd still only spoken once or twice before and even then only very briefly, but that same certainty I'd felt with Emma had come over me again.

A few days later, Kerry Katona from the Kittens rang me up and said, 'You going out tonight?' I was sitting with the other security men at this point so it was tricky, but I replied, 'Yes,' and Kerry said, 'Oh, well, we are and Tash is coming out too, by the way.' We all went out and had a wicked night. I spent a lot of time with Tash, but I was very wary of getting involved, so I didn't make any arrangements to see her again. I knew I already had feelings for this girl and I knew the sort of trouble this would cause professionally, so I guess I was just trying to avoid the undeniable draw I was feeling towards her. I kept telling myself, *I can't take this any further even though I really like this girl – I just can't.*

We didn't see each other for a couple of weeks after that great night and then one evening I was at a gay club with all the lads (on Sunday night everything was gay in London). Tash walked in and smashed me on the head with the back of the door, flattening me completely. I was stunned, lying on the floor in a daze, then as I regained focus, I looked up and she was standing over me.

From that second on we were with each other for three years.

We went back to my mate's club and carried on talking non-stop; we seemed to have so many things in common and stuff to talk about. I was listening to her and thinking, *Oh my God, I am really into this bird!* Then she kissed me and I swear to God, it was the best kiss I have ever had in my life! It was like I had kissed her a million times before. I can't explain it, it sounds ridiculously weird: it was almost like we had been together before. But there you go, that's how it felt.

We were always very wary of the repercussions,

should anyone find out. At one point Paul even asked me if I was seeing Natasha. It was so difficult at that time. One night we had a great time and stayed over at her hotel. The next morning I left and was walking down the road outside the hotel when the Kittens' tour manager drove past, saw me and blew his horn to say hello. I waved with a smile on my face, all the time thinking *Oh my God! He's bound to think that's too much of a coincidence...*

Inevitably Paul found out and I knew there was going to be trouble. He was very upset, which is fair enough because it is something that you just don't do in that job, despite what Kevin Costner's character might think. My first thought when Paul said he knew was that I was going to lose my job, one of the best I had ever had. The problem was me and Tash couldn't stop feeling the way we did just because of our jobs.

That December Tash came over to Ireland and we had the best Christmas ever. Mom and Dad were there, I had just started making it in London and was doing really well, I'd got a few nice clothes and was pumped up – 18-and-a-half stone! – and felt really on top of my game. Tash was there and we had great times, a beautiful family Christmas. So many times have I thought to myself, if only I could go back and live that all again. It was only about five days, but it was such a good time.

I travelled back to London in the New Year. Then, just after Christmas 2000, Paul rang me up and said, 'Listen, I'm sorry, Fran, but it's her or your job.'

I finished the call with Paul, rang Tash straight away and said, 'Look, I dunno what I am going to do here, they've just said to me, "Choose either Tash or the job."'

Almost immediately she started crying and as soon as she did, I said to myself, *Bollocks! I know what to do: it's simple.*

I said, 'I'll call you back in a minute,' and I rang Paul.

'Paul, I am sorry man, I am in love with this girl. I can't help it and I have to quit. I am so sorry to disappoint you and I'd like to thank you for the opportunity you gave me.'

At this point I hadn't even said those three words to Tash, so I rang her back and said, 'Babe, I just quit so we are staying together! I love you!' She started bawling her eyes out again – I don't think she could quite believe it.

From an outsider's point of view, it might seem rash to quit one of the top jobs in the business like that. In many ways it was the best job in the world. But you know what? It was such an easy decision to make when I heard Tash crying – all of the benefits of work seemed utterly irrelevant. I just wanted to be with her and if that meant a change of occupation, so be it.

As it happened, two days later Paul rang up again and asked, 'Can you come into the hotel for a chat? We've had a meeting with the band and they want to talk to you.' I was very embarrassed about it all at this stage because those lads had been very good to me and I had openly chosen to quit the job over this girl. To some observers, I hadn't acted professionally in the strict sense of the word. I went in and they told me that the band had taken a vote – and decided they wanted to keep me on! Nicky said he really liked me and he didn't care who I was dating, and that I could look after him. I sat there listening to this massive pop band talking to me, a band who could take their pick of the very finest security men in the world, and I have to say I was very humbled by it all; they certainly didn't have to do that at all. They could have had anyone they wanted. Amazingly, they took me out for a meal that night to welcome me back into the fold. To be honest, I was still embarrassed by it – I felt like I had let everyone down – but the way those lads treated me was so respectful, they were so cool, there was never a hint they had taken exception. Besides, their actions spoke for them.

When I met Tash I was going through one of the best periods of my life. It was amazing going out on the town. My crew of doormen was really tight and we could get into any club in town automatically. Every club we walked up to there'd be drinks, tables and just all-round amazing treatment. I had got through having no money and living in squalor and was finally making my own way, I was known about town and life was good. Now I had a beautiful woman with me, who I was madly in love with. I didn't take it for granted, though – it actually made me realise that no matter how bad things are, there is nothing that will put me on the ground.

Tash knew what my job was and didn't mind, although she was always concerned for me if something kicked off. One night I was in Pop with Tash and her little sister when this guy ran in and said, 'Fran, the two doormen are getting battered!' I ran out to find my mate Justin getting beaten up on these stairs, so I waded in and we sorted it out. I came back to Tash's table with blood sprayed all over my shirt and she was like, 'Oh my God!' 'Babe, don't worry,' I told her, 'it's not mine.'

Nothing was going to put Tash on the ground either, let me tell you that. When we went out with the crew, this petite Liverpudlian was the safest girl in the whole world. She was like the little princess of the whole group. She'd be partying with twenty-five massive doormen, who all protected her like a little sister. Thank God no man either tried it on with her or was rude to her, because he would not have been a pretty sight afterwards!

CHAPTER ELEVEN

# AROUND THE WORLD WITH WESTLIFE

The tour I did with Westlife was their first major international tour, and they loved it. We all worked incredibly hard – no one more so than the band – but there was a great rapport on the road, we had some brilliant times. They used to slag me off terrible, calling me a poser, really slaughtering me, though obviously I had to bite my lip and not slag them back. It was all in jest, of course, but they were merciless.

The tour was insanity from start to finish. When we arrived in the Philippines we were attacked at the airport. There were groups of fans who were pretty much acting as a mob – and the problem is that in the Far East, the fans don't just want to say hello to the band, they want to take their hands off. They want a piece of them as a souvenir.

I came around a corner of the airport to find Paul and the band being mobbed. We managed to get the boys to the safety of a car by throwing people off them, literally grabbing these teenagers and hurling them out of the way before they caused some real harm. When I turned around, though, Paul was getting assaulted by dozens of fans. I'd just found out that morning that the band and Paul had hidden a 30lb dumbbell in my bag for a few days – I was 18 stone and huge at this point, so to be honest I didn't even notice! I opened the bag, took out the dumbbell and waded into this crowd wailing like a banshee. There must have been twenty-five people kicking Paul so I thought to myself, *The first one who comes near me gets it!* They could see the look in my eye so they started backing off. I was shouting to Paul, 'Get in the car!' and at once we both started legging it for the exit. As we did, this mob charged after us, so I turned round, dumbbell held aloft in the air and screamed at them like something out of a battle movie. They all stopped dead in their tracks. I turned and ran, and then they carried on chasing me again. We dived into the car and sped off, hardly believing what had just happened.

It was only the beginning, though.

At one hotel, we had to lock off the entire floor so the band's personal safety wasn't at risk. Basically we were marooned on this floor for hours on end and I was bored off my tits. I was chatting with Mark and said, 'I really need to get some fresh air', so we went and found this balcony next to a fire door. We were standing there talking and relaxing when Mark accidentally leaned on the push-bar handle of the fire door, which flung open and he fell through... to find about one hundred and fifty fans staring in stunned silence at one of their idols, now only inches away from them. There was an odd pause while they registered what they were looking at. Then all hell broke loose.

I put my foot on the door to keep it open while I dragged Mark to safety, then I started trying to slam the door shut. As I said, I was a massive bloke at this point, but it was obvious there was no way I could hold the door for very long. I managed to get it within six inches of being shut and these hysterical fans were squeezing their faces through the gap, clamouring to get through, like Jack Nicholson in *The Shining*. It was pretty scary stuff, actually.

I realised I couldn't hold it any longer, so I turned to Mark and shouted, 'Run!' We went charging along this corridor, pissing ourselves laughing as we ran, and all the time these screaming fans were catching us up. It was so freaky. We turned a corner and there was a lift, so I pressed the button to call it.

Nothing happened.

'Come on, lift! Lift!'

We could hear them behind us getting closer.

Then, finally, there was a 'ping' and the lift door opened.

We dived inside and pushed the 'Close Doors' button just as the first fans turned the corner to see the lift door. Before we had a chance to breath a sigh of relief, instead of going up to the sanctuary of our isolated floor, the lift started going down to reception – where we knew for a fact that two thousand fans were camped out. You can imagine Mark and myself standing in that silent lift, heading down to the lobby, knowing what was waiting for us.

'Oh my God! This can't be happening.'

Ping!

The lift door opened and two thousand teenage fans' faces looked up to see Mark from Westlife standing in a lift, in reception, stranded.

I was next to Mark frantically pushing the button to take us up to our floor, muttering, 'Fucking hell, come on, come on, come on!'

Suddenly the hubbub of chat in the lobby was broken by an ear-piercing scream as thousands of fans shouted at us in unison and started to run to the lift. The doors were closing so slowly and these kids were running so fast, everything seemed to be happening in slow motion. We were just standing there waiting like condemned men; it was hilarious and frightening at the same time. Literally, with the first fan about five feet away, the lift doors finally slammed shut and we headed upwards away from the insanity to the safety of our hotel room. I turned to Mark, half-laughing, breathing heavily and said, 'Er, let's keep this to ourselves, shall we?'

Even leaving a hotel to get to a show or simply going out for the night was a major security operation. One time in Jakarta, the boys wanted to go for a meal and the only safe route was through the kitchens. As we walked through these working kitchens, fans started falling out of cupboards and were throwing themselves on the band. They'd somehow managed to squeeze themselves into the tiniest of spaces and waited for hours on the off chance the band might come that way. I almost felt sorry for them as I pushed them back into each cupboard, shut the door and ushered the band past. Lunatics!

Following one show in the Philippines, we all leapt into these jeeps to head back to the hotel and after a few hundred yards, suddenly someone asked, 'Where's Brian?' It transpired he was still stuck in the dressing room, so I jumped out of the car, ran back to the venue, got hold of him, chaperoned him past hundreds of fans and bundled him into the car. As soon as I had shut the door with me still outside on the road the car started to drive off so I started running after it, shouting for them to stop. I looked around and there must have been five hundred screaming fans stampeding down the road after me, I felt like I was literally running for my life. As I got level with the car, the back window opened and I jumped in, but by then some fans had caught up with us and they pulled my shoes off. I was lucky that was all they grabbed, because let me tell you, they don't let go.

The Far East was definitely the most mental for fans, but the UK had some real diehards too. There was this one kid who we called Stan the Mad Fan, from Birmingham. One day we came out of the Hilton in Birmingham and, as usual, Stan was sitting on the hotel steps waiting for the band. We got in the tour bus to drive to the capital for *CD:UK* and when we got off the coach at the Hilton in London, Stan was already there, sitting on the step.

We did *CD:UK* and headed off in the tour bus back up to Birmingham and as we did, someone spotted Stan cycling after us through all the London back-streets. He rode for miles and miles before we finally lost him somewhere around Waterloo. As we drove off into the distance, I looked back and Stan was sitting on his bike waving at us. We drove all the way back to Birmingham, got out of the tour bus only to find Stan sitting on the same step waiting for us again.

One time Westlife were coming out of their hotel up in Glasgow when there was a massive rush by the fans. This young girl fell over and smashed her head open on the kerb. She was really badly cut, her whole face seemed to have fallen down over her head, she was in a real state and losing blood fast. I picked her up and with Paul we got her to a hospital as quickly as we could – she had something like a hundred emergency stitches to fix her up. The lads went to see her the next day and she even spoke to a magazine about it all, telling them how grateful her parents were to me – it was really nice. She seemed to take a real shine to me and said some very nice things. And she still thought it was OK about the scar, because of the way she got it!

It wasn't just the fans who could be extreme, though. Some of the overseas bodyguards we had to work with were wild too. Like 'Ivan the Terrible', for example. This security guy chaperoned people in South Africa and over there, the band needed heavily armed bodyguards, but we weren't licensed for weapons. So extra bodyguards had to be hired. We walked out of our hotel and Ivan was sitting on the bonnet of his car – he was about eight feet tall and had a sub-machine-gun strapped around his massive shoulders. 'I am Ivan the Terrible,' he said as he crushed my fingers with his handshake, handing me a business card, which showed him exactly as we found him, sitting astride his car carrying an Uzi. It turned out he was an absolute gentleman actually, a lovely lad. The gun culture in South Africa was shocking, though – guns everywhere. Even the car park attendants had pump-action shotguns.

The Security there were lunatics: one time the road out of the airport was jammed solid, the traffic was terrible. We were all tired and hot so I turned to the security guy attached to us and asked, 'Hey, is there anything we can do to get out of this road?' thinking maybe there was a short-cut or similar. He looked at me and said, 'Yes! Sir!' like a soldier, then proceeded to wind his window down, pull out a double-barrel shotgun and smash the butt of it against the next-door car! He was screaming and swearing, hanging out of the window banging all these cars with his shotgun, it was nuts! I asked, 'What the fuck are you doing?' but he just carried on. Not surprisingly, the cars all moved out of the way.

At the time, I was really big and my jaw dead square. When we got to Manila, we were met by Marines, who were to escort us. As we walked out, I could see most of them looking at me in particular, which obviously felt very odd. Then this huge marine walked over to me and said, 'Oh my God! It *is* you, Jean-Claude Van Damme!' They were all mentallers, real hard bastards, but I could do no wrong because they thought I was Jean-Claude!

As usual, when we got to the hotel, we were pretty much locked up on an isolated floor. The Security and Marines had brought a few of their families down there and were basically living on the floor with the band. The day before we left we were standing in the corridor and some of these people came over to me and said, 'Jean-Claude! Do a kick! Do a kick!' It seemed a shame to disappoint them so I took one of their snacks off them – a bag of nuts – and got this guy to hold it six feet in the air. I then twisted round and did a back kick, smashing this bag to pieces, but not touching his hand at all. They were all like, 'Wow! Jean-Claude! Jean-Claude! Jean-Claude!'

When those shows were done, we headed off to the airport but got stopped on the way by the Police. One came up and knocked on the window. He took his helmet off and passed it into the car.

'Can you sign the helmet?'

I took the helmet and passed it to one of the boys.

'No, you!' the policeman said.

'What?'

'You, Jean-Claude.'

At this point, the public relations guy from the record company leaned over to my ear and said, 'Mate, sign the helmet, sign the fucking helmet!' As soon as I had, the policeman put it back on his head and said, 'I will escort you to the airport personally.' Then he and his mate drove ahead of us with the lights and sirens on all the way to the terminal. It was bizarre.

Driving from Sun City to Cape Town to Johannesburg we got to see a lot of the countryside and the poverty by the side of the road was incredible. The shanty towns were appalling. I don't want to sound corny, but it does make you think what lucky bastards we are – you think you have problems sometimes but we are so lucky. The lifestyles we have grown accustomed to compared to the shit that those people endure – we are just worlds apart. Some of the houses were simply a piece of tin and a net across a door. It was desperate. Compared to the madness of a pop band's tour, it seemed like a different universe.

When we got to Beirut we needed more armed guards. En route to the venue, we turned down this darkened road only to find a gun fight in progress: we were about to drive down a sniper's alley. All six cars stopped in a line, then suddenly there was a hush and the bullets stopped. We drove quickly through between these two opposite sets of buildings, while the gunfire ceased momentarily to allow this oversized black convoy to slide through. Then as soon as the final vehicle was past, the gunfire started to rip across the streets once more.

Yet we had a job to do, and needed to press on. Of course, the insanity went up a notch when we got to the actual shows. In Hong Kong, Westlife did their first concert singing 'in the round' (that's when the audience sit in a big circle all around the band, rather than in front of a stage). It was a brilliant show, but halfway through Brian ran to the edge of the stage and jumped into the crowd – I have never run so fast in my whole life! I ran the whole way across the stage, took a massive leap over the railings and landed halfway up the steps to get to him. People were so scared seeing me bearing down on them, they just ran out of the way.

The first time we were in Seoul, I had to debrief a hundred soldiers who were needed to keep the crowd in order. I stood on this block, shouting out my plans for the security, while next to me this soldier translated, barking out the orders to these massed ranks. It was such a bizarre situation to find myself in – these were people who kill for a living and I was just a bodyguard. They were all looking at me with great respect and, because I was so into my job, I had no problem telling them what to do. At the end, they all stamped their feet to attention and a hundred soldiers' voices shouted, 'Yes, Mr Fran!' I nearly shit myself.

I tell you what though, the band needed that level of security – it was crazy. In Seoul one of the venues had over-sold this massive football stadium, which held about fifty thousand people, so it was pandemonium. That single gig was one of the hardest days' work I've ever done in my life. The band was not allowed on stage until every single person was sitting down and thousands of them were milling around, trying to find seats. It was absolute chaos. I ended up diving into the crowd, trying to find everyone a seat. It must have been about 120 degrees and incredibly humid, so I was sweating like a pig!

One of the other Security, Anton, was up on stage, trying to placate the audience, who were getting restless for the show to start. Eventually, it came down to this one middle-aged man, there with his family, who was the only person without a seat. He alone was holding up a concert for around fifty thousand people.

I said to him, 'Look, you are going to have to go to the back and use a seat up there. You are going to have to move, I'm afraid.'

He simply said, 'No.'

The crowd was starting to get very restless.

Now I was really sweating.

I looked at him, looked round at Anton and the crowd, then with a final burst of energy, picked him up over my shoulder and started marching towards the spare seat at the back of the auditorium. I felt something hit me and when I looked down, all his kids were kicking me in the legs as I walked, shouting at me and screaming.

I finally got to the seat and put him down gently in it. As I did so, I turned round to go back towards the stage and the entire crowd stood up and gave me the most amazing ovation. Anton was killing himself laughing, saying to the crowd, 'Give it up for Mr Buzz Lightyear, ladies and gentlemen!'

You might think he'd just thought of that nickname because of what I'd done, but actually we all had our own pseudonyms that we used to check into hotels. Mine was 'Buzz Lightyear'. Normally, it was all a bit of a laugh, but on one particular day on the tour, that false name was the cause of one more problem at the end of the most ridiculously disastrous day ever.

All the lads had already got on their onward flight for the next show and it was down to me to do the early shift to take Nicky's girlfriend Georgina to the airport too. After that, because of the connections, I had to fly from Birmingham to Denmark, then Denmark to Switzerland. I was shattered so I blacked out on the plane, only to wake up later to find all these air hostesses standing over me.

'Are you an American football player? Or baseball?' asked one of them.

'What? Er, no. Where am I? I need to get a connecting flight.'

'Oh my God... you are joking...'

I looked around and there was no one else on the plane. I ran from one side of the massive airport in Copenhagen to the other, only to find my gate already closed and I had just missed my flight. I was begging them to let me through but they said they weren't allowed to, when all of a sudden the gate re-opened because they had to off-load some luggage. I ran down that corridor to the plane in seconds, I tell you.

Anton had told me that my hotel in Switzerland was the nearest one to the airport. I came through Arrivals and switched my mobile on, but the battery was dead. I went to the cash machine to get some local currency and it made a few odd noises and took my card. Later I realised I was putting the wrong pin number in there – one of those days. So within ten minutes of landing, I had got no mobile and no money.

I am so used to using my mobile I don't actually remember anyone's phone numbers any more, so I collect called to Tash, the only number I could recall, who in turn had to ring Anton, who then rang me back on a public payphone in the airport! Anton said I was booked into the Copthorne, so I walked outside to get a cab.

The problem was, the hotel near to the airport was not a Copthorne. I asked the cabbie how far it was to my hotel and he said, 'Miles away!' I told him I had no cash but could pay him when we arrived. It took an hour and twenty minutes and cost a fortune. I asked him to wait outside while I went to check in at Reception.

I walked up to the desk, looking like death warmed up from exhaustion, and asked, 'Can I check in, please?'

'Of course, sir. What is your name, please?'

'Mr Buzz Lightyear.'

She looked at me strangely and typed this into her computer.

'Sorry sir, we have no booking for a Mr Buzz Lightyear.'

'Are you sure? I've just spoken to the person who booked it and he said it was all sorted.'

'Can I check I heard your name right, sir?'

'Yes, Lightyear, Mr, Buzz.'

'No, sorry, sir, there is no booking. Were you staying with anyone else?'

'Yes, Britney Spears, Michael Jackson and MC Hammer.'

At this point, I noticed the hotel security guard start to move over to the desk.

In desperation I gave them Anton's actual surname but that wasn't there either. I told them the name of the hotel and the lady said, 'Sorry sir, that is the other Copthorne, just down the road from here.'

I was in the wrong bloody hotel!

I can be quite accident-prone at times. Although all the Security was pretty much on duty 24/7 for three months, we did get the occasional night off. I got lost in Japan. We had three days on, two days off, I was wound up and wanted to blow off some steam so we went to some mad nightclubs and had a great time. But when I came out into this busy Tokyo street I was on my own and couldn't see anyone I knew. I reached for my phone but I had lost that again too (I lose a phone about three times a year). I had no idea where I was, there were no signs in English, of course, and I couldn't speak a word of Japanese.

So what did I do?

I rang me da.

I got him to ring Paul Higgins, they worked out where I must be from the description I gave and sent someone to get me!

Bizarrely, MTV offered me a job out there. I'd been with the band for various interviews and one of the girls at MTV approached the lads, asked about me, then came over and asked: 'Would you be interested in presenting a show?' I thought she was ripping the piss. But they were deadly serious; in fact they really wanted me. They offered me an apartment, great money and a car. I would never have walked off a tour with the lads, though; I had a job to do. I didn't think about it too seriously, but it was very funny – I got abused by Westlife for ages over that!

Occasionally, it was the stars needing to be kept in check more than the fans. One time I was with Westlife at the Brit Awards and the day was going swimmingly, everything was running exactly to plan. Then someone said they'd heard Eminem was planning to invade the stage. So I went off looking for his security blokes and was pointed in the direction of these two massive lumps of men. They looked so big you almost expected their arms and legs could extend at any minute to make them even bigger, it was surreal. I was still 18 stone, but they absolutely dwarfed me; I felt like a little boy standing next to them. Knowing American security can be quite abrasive, I was prepared for the worst, but I got chatting and explained my concerns and, sure enough, there was no stage invasion. Any time they are in London, they come down to my club. It's the same with Justin Timberlake's guys. I always look after them – and he seems like a nice kid.

The main Westlife tour was eight months, I think, from start to finish – a long old time. But I absolutely loved that job: it was the highest level of the security game within entertainment, personal bodyguard to a celebrity. I loved it. There was only one time when I really didn't want to go in to work. We'd been in London and the lads had finished a gig at GAY in the West End. We were driving along Tottenham Court Road and Mark said he wanted a drink. We pulled up at some lights and he jumped out, so I had to follow him.

I'm glad I did, because we had a mental night and bumped into the England rugby player Lawrence Dallaglio and a few other rugby lads. Eventually Mark got tired and I was happy to head home because I had an early start ahead of a show the next night. As we got in the car to drive home, Dallaglio jumped in the back and said, 'Don't go home yet! Come for a drink with me!' So I took Mark back and we all went back out. I have to tell you I can drink as well as the next man, but that night we got ossified! We were so pissed, steaming drunk.

When we finally decided to head home, with the dawn only a couple of hours away, me and Lawrence jumped into the back of the car and as we drove off we could hear this metallic scraping noise. At first we couldn't tell what it was, but then we realised it was the axle of the car scraping along the road because we were such a weight in the back.

Sadly for my night's sleep, just as we got out of the car we bumped into even more England players and went out again to a club called The Church. I was bolloxed. Finally I got back to the hotel, realised I'd lost my phone again and crawled into bed. I'd just shut my eyes when the phone rang and it was Paul Higgins asking if I was ready for work. 'I'm already in work, now fuck off!' was all I could say as I dragged myself out of the still, cold bed. It was all Lawrence Dallaglio's fault!

# CHAPTER TWELVE

# THE BEST OF TIMES

I was with Westlife for about eighteen months. Tash was on the road a lot during that time with Atomic Kitten, so we were spending a lot of time apart; however, we often chatted about living together during our long international phone calls. One night Tash rang me up and said she had been thinking about getting a new house with some girls, but had then changed her mind, and instead asked me: 'Can we move in together?' I was shocked but said, 'Yeah! Why not?' I don't know why, but Tash has always had that effect on me. So when I came back, we moved in together.

The first stage of the tour was the European leg, which included thirteen Wembley Arenas, then we had a bit of a break before flying out again to the Far East and farther afield. That's when me and Tash got engaged – we'd been dating about five months at the time. It was a deadly night. We were in Tenerife and I just got down and asked her on the beach, a lovely moment.

I'd thought I'd be gone for four weeks or so with the next Westlife tour, but when I got to the airport and asked, 'How long are we away for?' Paul replied, 'Three months!' Tash freaked, and I wasn't too pleased either! We managed to see each other quite a lot, though, despite the distance. For example, the Kittens flew out to Israel for a show that coincided with Westlife dates, and it was great to see her then. But I can't deny that lifestyle was very hard on the relationship. The phone calls, the different time zones, the hectic schedules, it was very hard – brutal. I don't know if we could do that now.

I'll be honest with you: I'd fallen madly head over heels in love with her by now. Anything that jeopardised that was very frightening to me. One thing I regret almost as much as anything I have ever done was a night when I was out on the town and had had too much to drink. I should have headed home but I was pissed and not thinking straight. One of my friends said, 'Tash is on the phone,' and I said, 'Tell her I am not here' – not realising that he was holding the phone to my ear so she heard me say it.

I didn't say that because I was up to anything I shouldn't have been, I was just pissed and not thinking. But when it hit home I was terrified I might lose her. I'm afraid I freaked out, picked up this mate and threw him over a table. What makes this all the worse is that the next morning I couldn't remember any of it. Sometimes you drink too much; it's as simple as that. It bothered me for ages, still does, to be honest. I don't bullshit myself –

a lot of people can do that, but if I fuck up, I take it really hard. I go over things in my head and I can be really tough on myself when I've done wrong. That was a serious mistake and to this day it remains one of the most regrettable things I've done.

We were in our apartment in London and Tash was late for her period.

We did the test.

It was positive.

Woah!

My life had just totally changed in a few seconds. We were both really happy, 'We are going to be parents!' We'd been together for about two years at this point and had talked about children, but hadn't expected the news that soon, so we were overjoyed. When we told our parents they were so excited – not least because for both families it would be the first grandkid. My dad Dermot was stuck for words, as indeed was Tash's dad.

I was only 24; Tash was just 19. The first time we went for a scan, it was incredible, looking at the tiny person on the screen. It's something that happens to people every day, of course, but it felt absolutely amazing. The whole period of the pregnancy and birth was completely mad – we were both working so hard, Tash's band was very popular and always running at ninety miles an hour. When the tour ended I had finished working with

Westlife but was doing security consultancy then preparing to launch my first London club, Click (of which more later!). We never had a spare minute and as such, looking back now, the pregnancy simply flew by. For a bloke pregnancy is a weird time: the woman goes through some mad-ass shit and even though you are there for them, at times you feel like someone tied you onto the end of a tractor and dragged you across a field. You just never know when the next bump is coming. I have to honest: it was a pretty trying time.

After we told our parents, we didn't want to tell anyone else; we really wanted to keep the news private, but it did get out to the papers. The first few times we went looking for baby clothes, we were sneaking around the shop and as soon as the woman behind the counter recognised Tash and myself, we said, 'It's not for us, it's for a friend!' Ridiculous, really.

Tash was in labour for ten hours. She was two weeks overdue, and had been eating curries and having acupuncture to bring the baby on. It was a Friday night and I was at a business meeting with Rav from *News of the World* and a few other people. After we had finished they were trying to tempt me out for the night. I was shattered and wanted to get back home to be with Tash, so I politely declined. Just as well.

I went home, got in bed and we put on this really shit video – *Brotherhood of Wolves*, I will never forget it. After a while, my tiredness caught up with me and I fell asleep. The next thing I know, Tash was nudging my arm saying, 'Fran! Fran! My waters have just broke!' Now about fifteen times through the pregnancy's later stages, Tash had woken me up, thinking the baby was on its way, so when she did this time I was like, 'Yeah, whatever!'

'No, really! Fran, the baby is on its way!'

'Oh my God!'

I was out of the bed in a flash and getting dressed. Tash's mom and dad were staying with us so I knocked on the door and shouted, 'Tash is having the baby!' It was total pandemonium, running around the flat getting ready. Tash was all ready to go in no time but me and her dad were ironing shirts and she was at the door shouting, 'Get in the car!'

We had a really good time in hospital, a total laugh. I remember thinking how beautiful Tash looked. The bump was absolutely enormous, but she suited being pregnant, she looked stunning and oozed that natural glow mothers-to-be get. For the first two hours of the labour, this woman down the hall was wailing and screaming, but Tash was so brave, she was just sitting there, seemingly totally relaxed.

The labour was coming on rather slowly and Tash had an epidural to help with the pain, but the doctor was not convinced it was happening quickly enough. Then Josh's head started to get squashed and he seemed in distress... it was a terrifying moment, I couldn't do anything and was standing by helplessly, completely petrified (now I knew exactly how my dad felt all those years ago when I had arrived in similar circumstances). So the decision was made to perform a Caesarean section.

There was no way I was going to let Tash go into theatre on her own, so I got them to give me some surgeon's robes and headed in there with them, looking like an enormous, pumped-up Dr Kildare with the masks and all the gear. I tell you what, having seen what went on, I have to say that Tash is a very brave bird – in fact, any woman who gives birth is. The epidural had kicked in, so fortunately she could feel very little and we were just holding hands and looking at one another as they performed what is, after all, a major operation.

Anticipating that first cry was amazing, but when Josh finally came out, we just hugged each other and Tash burst into tears. I didn't cry myself, but I was very emotional. They handed the umbilical cord and a pair of surgical scissors to me, but I chose not to cut it. As soon as they had cut the cord, they handed Josh to me and I held him over a bowl and started washing him down.

The first time I looked at him I thought *Oh My God!* What a moment in life, you will never get it again, your first kid being born. Josh was obviously crying but I just held him to my chest and whispered quietly into his tiny ear. He went tranquil almost straight away – I put a lot of that down to having spoken to him in Tash's belly all the time throughout the pregnancy. I held him close and spoke softly to him for a while and it was just beautiful. Tash wasn't well enough to hold him straight away, but I brought him down to her face and she was bawling! A deadly day – I go funny even thinking about it.

Tash's dad George is mixed blood and he'd been winding me up for ages saying 'It skips a few generations, this could be the one!' And when Josh was handed to me from Tash's stomach, he was seriously dark – I looked and thought *Oh my God, George is going to have a laugh!* I wrapped Josh in a white blanket and took him to show Tash's mom, who was outside the operation room.

We stayed at the hospital itself, which was just as well because Tash was in a jock for some time. That first morning, I took her some breakfast, still dressed in my Dr Kildare robes – I really liked them! I was walking through the corridor at one point and as I passed this door, a lady in the room shouted, 'Excuse me, doctor!' I didn't look like a real doctor for long, though – I didn't realise you had to give the outfit back so I cut the trousers into shorts and cut the arms off the T-shirt!

Towards the end of that first day, they were both dozing off. I was almost delirious from tiredness and desperate for a wash so one of the nurses said I could go down and take a shower. The light in the room was on a timer switch so I got in and started showering down. Then all of a sudden the light went off, and it was instantly pitch-black dark. I was thrashing around trying to find the light switch when I felt a cord, so I pulled it. Nothing happened, so I pulled it again. And again, and again. But still there was total darkness. So I started to try to make my way out of the room, fumbling around naked for my towel.

Suddenly the door burst open and two nurses crashed in shouting, 'Are you alright?' I'd pulled an emergency cord. It was like a cartoon, me standing there bollock naked going, 'I'm sorry! I'm sorry!' and them standing opposite me shouting, 'Aaaahhh!'

We'd found out that some of the Press was trying to get pictures, but fortunately we were in a different hospital to the one they thought we were in. Nonetheless, as we walked out of the hospital with Josh in his little carrycot, I went straight into security mode, looking around, scanning the corridors, checking the doorways. We put a blanket over his head but when we got in the lift, this woman looked down and cooed over him, and I was like, 'Do you mind?' Tash and her mom were laughing at me and telling me to take it easy. If that was scary, driving him home was worse – being in a car and effectively trusting someone else with this brand-new little life that you have to protect. I was very relieved when we finally got him home.

Tash had wanted to get the nursery all done beforehand and with the lateness of the birth we were able to get it all ready. But what a state! She'd gone out and bought all this stuff for Josh's room, but it was down to me to put it up. Let me tell you, I am not a DIY person. It took me forever to put a border up and then my attention turned to this mirror. I must have drilled about eighteen holes in the wall to put this one screw in for the mirror – it took me ages! Then Tash walked in and asked, 'Why on earth have you put a mirror up over the baby-changing table?' Not a good idea. I moved it to another wall, which was just as well because two days later there was an enormous crash in the middle of the night. 'That's the mirror, isn't it?' I said in abject resignation.

It wasn't just Josh's room either. Tash wanted to paint all our gaff so while she was away working for a few days I bought all the paint and did the entire flat in between work. The place had all these weird high ceilings, so it took me five days to finish. I was sick of it by the end.

Then Tash came back from her trip, walked in and said, 'I don't like the colour.'

'Don't say that to me!'

I painted it all again.

# CHAPTER THIRTEEN

# CLICK

As if having just become a father two days previously wasn't enough, I opened my first London nightclub, Click, two days after Josh was born. How did it all come about? Well, one night I was doing the door at this place called Stork Rooms. I had a chat with one of the owners and he asked me, 'So, what do you want to do?' 'I want to open my own club,' I told him. I was conscious that if all I ever did was DJ or door work, then I would be limiting myself. My voracious appetite for new experiences and new skills demanded that I spread my wings.

The owner came to me a few days later and asked, 'Will you come down to the office? I want to have a chat with you.' He explained he'd got this venue in mind so I went to see the place and talked through the deal. I did some research, but to be honest I already knew what I wanted to do, what way I would go with the size, the design and so on. Even so, you need to know all about your location and what that will allow you to achieve, because certain locations will make things hard. There are so many factors to consider – what capacity you are going to work with, what days are going to work, what structure you are going to build inside and what it will look like outside, how you execute the PR... Fortunately, it all comes naturally to me. I feel like I've been involved in clubs all my life, so it feels like common sense, to be honest.

We called the club Click. We were in our apartment with Tash and her sister Georgina watching telly and trying to come up with a name for the club. We were messing with the Sky remote and on the screen it said 'Click on the red button to go interactive...' I looked at her and she was thinking the same as me: 'Click! What a deadly name for a nightclub.' So that was that.

The club had been a dishevelled gay club on Wardour Street that was about to be closed down, but I announced, 'Give me a box and two weeks and I will turn it into something special.' We closed the back corridor down, and the very next thing I did was to cover the opening corridor with floor-to-ceiling mirrors and red carpet so by the time you actually got into the club, you already felt like a superstar. Apart from that, we didn't actually do that much. Once you were in the club, there was a DJ box to the side on the left, a side stage where people used to sit and a big dance floor; through another level there was a massive bar then a door for the VIP room. By that stage in my professional life in London, the assets I could bring to the table for a nightclub were pretty sizeable – the connections, the celebrities, the experience. It represented a pretty potent package, so we were all very excited.

On the opening night we threw a surprise party for Tash – all the Kittens came down, Westlife, Ronan Keating and his wife, plus loads of our other friends, a whole crowd of people who really supported me well. That first night was a storming party, it got us plenty of press coverage and the very next evening when we opened the doors there were two hundred and fifty people in a queue down the street waiting to get in.

Click was mental. I had some of the best parties of my life there. Along with my business partners I had a third share in the place. On top of Click and doing my part with Josh, I was running the security on and off for another small club in London at the same time, so this was one very busy period. I loved Click; it was my very own little Studio 54. Everybody who went to Click will have a story about it being one of the best nights of their lives.

Celebrities poured through the door; the queues were endless. When a big name was in town, they came down to the club: Ja Rule, Beenie Man, Justin Timberlake, Janet Jackson, Christina Aguilera, *NSYNC, the Backstreet Boys. Some nights these people would be sitting in one room: all the cool people. I'd be sitting back with two bottles of champagne watching all this evolve in front of my eyes. It was an insane time for me, but the best of times too. I bumped into the producer and artist Pharrell Williams one night in a hotel and he told me he wanted to go out clubbing. We headed down to Click, where I had a live percussion band on at the time. He asked if he could go up on stage and play, so off he went and started playing the bongos while the crowd went nuts. Then he turned to the DJ and asked him to cut the music and sang Justin Timberlake's debut solo hit record, 'Like I Love You', the whole track live, while everyone in Click watched in awe.

People sometimes ask me what it's like to work with celebrities. It's pretty straightforward, to be honest. When I meet a celebrity I treat them with respect. I don't get star-struck. When I first arrived in London, I had no take on celebrity, I'd come in from Ireland and I just started to meet them as part of my job. I didn't really pay much attention to it all. If a celebrity wants to talk to me they will come and talk to me. If not, then I let them have a nice night alone. I can honestly say the only celebrity who has ever made me feel star-struck is Jack Nicholson. When I saw him I didn't know where to put myself – he's such a legend and, I am pleased to say from my brief experience of meeting him, a very nice man too.

One of the downsides of entertaining American superstars is that their security can be very heavy-handed. One incident of note happened at another club I'd worked at, when a photographer caused a commotion by trying to take pictures of Wyclef Jean from The Fugees. Now Wyclef's security man is called 'The Beast'.

He is called The Beast for a reason: a giant of a man, he absolutely towers over everyone, all topped off with these amazing dreadlocks. Anyway, this situation started kicking off and progressed very quickly, so a lot of doormen came over to try to sort it out. I was in the back having a massive punch-up, helped by some other doormen, when a fellow security guy accidentally grabbed The Beast's brother. Naturally The Beast waded in to help his sibling. I turned around while the punches were being thrown at me to find my mate Paul having a punch-up with The Beast! I jumped on The Beast's back and said, 'He's with me, he's my mate!' I'd met The Beast a few times fortunately, so he took my word for it and let him go. Then me, The Beast and Paul turned on these troublesome punters. No matter what his nickname might suggest, The Beast is a gentleman, a classic bloke.

We had a lot of footballers and sportsmen down at Click too. In fact, the partying was so extreme that at one point my business partner and accountant – both Tottenham Hotspur supporters – sat me down after a meeting and said, 'Fran, the Spurs team are not allowed in here any more.' Only the week before, Robbie Keane – a great bloke – had been partying with me and dancing on tables, drinking vodka and having a great time. My partners were worried I would show their team such a good time their results might actually suffer.

It was not so much the celebrities but friends who came and partied that was so fantastic about Click. For me, Click was about all my friends, from pop stars to doormen to bar staff to PR people to lawyers to actresses and so on – they all came together under one roof and had a great party! Many nights after the club had closed we would have a private after-party into the small hours. We had some deadly times when Brian McFadden would get up to sing something, then the Kittens would get up. We'd all be dancing, partying, Justin Timberlake got up one night and was singing on the microphone, and all the time I would be surveying this from behind the champagne at my private table. I have to be honest: it felt bloody good!

One night, my best friend Rachel had got very drunk and we lost all track of her. We searched high and low for her in the club, but she was nowhere to be seen. So, assuming she'd headed home, we locked the club up for the night. Next morning, we found her curled up asleep under the DJ box! And what's worse, she had no memory of getting down there. Another one of my other mates, Rob, who is a cop now, got very pissed and insisted on continuing the party after Click closed. We often left Click as a big gang and took over a restaurant somewhere nearby. That night, Rob was in a bad way but when he heard we were moving on, he asked, 'Can I come to the party?' I looked at him and could tell how drunk he was, so I put my finger on his forehead, touched him and he collapsed backwards. I stood over him laughing out loud and said, 'You are too fucked, you can't come!'

I used to drive around the West End in my Voyager

picking people up from the clubs and then bring them back to my club. I literally used to come running across the club and jump into the VIP room – it was mental! That VIP room was legendary, let me tell you, there was a totally different buzz in there. People still tell me stories about the first time they got into the Click VIP room. It only really held eighty people, but one night I looked around and there must have been at least one hundred and fifty in there, people were stuck together like Superglue. It didn't bother anyone, they were just jumping up and down in unison, but I looked out at this sea of heads going up and down and realised the VIP room was getting too mad. So I walked down and sat on the other side of the room near the end of the bar where no one ever used to sit. I looked at this area for a few minutes and thought, *I could turn this into a VIP room as well.*

The next day we bought a £140 curtain and put it up – one new VIP room! Who says nightclubs have to be expensive? That night I went and sat in there and word soon spread that this was the new VIP room. All of a sudden, the old VIP room was dead and this new one packed! This previously unused area of the club was now the place to be.

The frenzy to get in the new VIP room was immediately as frantic as it had been before. One night a group of people kept trying to get in, but with no luck. Eventually, this one guy came running at full pelt through the crowds and jumped through the curtain –

you could see the relief on his face: he was in the VIP room! The problem was he'd brought the curtain down off the wall with him; the clubbers in the VIP room abruptly came face to face with those who were not. Ludicrous, really: the best VIP room in London and it was all because of a £140 curtain!

It got to the stage at Click where celebrities would pour through the door most nights and I became used to seeing some of the most famous faces in music and entertainment sipping champagne and having a great time in my club. One night I took a phone call from an old friend at another club.

'Hey Fran, listen, I've got Prince here but he's not happy with how the night is turning out and he wants to move on. Can you sort this out?' she asked me.

'OK, no problem, send him over, babe.'

'Yeah, but listen, Fran, Prince is one of those people who really likes getting looked after – that's why I've rung you.'

'Babe, I will be waiting for him at the door myself.'

So Prince came straight over to Click. I met him at the door as I had promised, said, 'Hello sir, nice to meet you,' shook his hand and started to lead him down to the club. Then someone said, 'By the way, Fran, he's come with a few people,' and when I looked behind him, there must have been one hundred and fifty people in his entourage!

We went downstairs and started having a chat and a drink. Prince is a born-again Christian who totally abstains from alcohol and he seemed like a very nice gentleman. Now, I hadn't noticed but we were sitting next to this huge, brightly lit mural I'd had put up on one wall that depicted some sexual imagery, including a fair number of willies and tits. After a while, Prince was beginning to look a little uncomfortable; he leaned over to my ear and asked me, 'Is it possible you could turn that mural around or take it down, please?'

I had promised I would look after Prince, so nothing was too much trouble. And, if you think of it from a business point of view, it can only be a good thing to have celebrities of that status in your club. Now, I knew I couldn't take the mural down because of how it was hung; but I also knew that if I turned the lights off around it, the club would be so dark he wouldn't be able to see the offending images at all. So I said, 'No problem, no problem, just wait here a moment.'

I walked out of the main club area and down through the bowels of the building until I got behind the wall where Prince was sitting and this mural was back-lit. I tried to unplug the lights, switch them off, dim them, everything, but it just wasn't happening. I could see Prince and the rest of the club partying away, oblivious to me having this crisis behind the scenes – not what you would expect from the guy behind the capital's premier VIP nightclub!

In desperation, I took hold of the main electricity cable that fed these lights and ripped it out of the wall. So now I was standing with a live cable in one hand, holding the back of the mural in place with the other and with

Prince about two feet away. I managed to attract the attention of a doorman, called him over, then said, 'Here, hold this!' and gave him the cable, adding: 'Be careful with that, it's live!'

I radioed for some help and left him waiting for back-up while I headed back to Prince's table. Before I got there, I mopped the sweat off my brow, took a deep breath, sat down and said, 'There you go, no problem at all. How you doing?'

He was much more relaxed after that and we started having a good old chat about all sorts; I found him to be friendly and very interesting. Then, to my amazement, he leaned over to my ear again and said, 'Listen, would you mind if I DJ-ed?' Like a reflex reaction, I said, 'Hold it right there, I will be back in two seconds.' Prince DJ-ing in my club? I could barely believe what I'd just heard.

I walked around to the DJ booth and spoke to the resident DJ, who was totally cool with the idea. We got out a big selection of records then I went and fetched Prince. It was so exciting; I have to tell you. Thinking back to that first shift at Night Owls for instance, then fast-forwarding to this evening, escorting Prince up to DJ at my own central London nightclub, the scale of the journey has never been lost on me. Never!

People always had a brilliant time at Click. That night was no different, it was absolutely packed and the atmosphere was superb. The crowd could see there was a change of DJ in progress, so they were craning their necks to see who was next. Prince is quite a small bloke but then suddenly his head popped up in the DJ box... the crowd stopped dancing and you could almost see this collective thought, *Oh my God! That's Prince about to DJ!* People could not believe what they were seeing. Then he put on his first record and the club *exploded*. I was sitting at my table, sipping a bottle of the best champagne, watching all of this... You could say I had quite a large smile on my face. When the night was over, Prince came up to me and said it had been a great night, that I was very respectful and that his security thought I was a gentleman. The next day, his impromptu DJ set made all the tabloids.

During this time, pictures of me started appearing in the papers. For me it was very odd. Everyone knew me for being a deadly scrapper, sorting shit out and always making sure everyone was alright. Within the space of three weeks of my first nightclub opening, it was a big sensation in London – and I could see that fact being newsworthy too. I could afford to look the part because I was taking good money out of that nightclub. I'd got this tag of 'Fran the Man' and I was definitely a face around town, but I thought, *Once a bouncer, always a bouncer.* I vividly remember the very first article the papers wrote about me. It was very positive, this 'Irish-bouncer-made-good' angle. I just couldn't stop laughing, to be honest.

I roared with laughter when they ran a story saying me and Tash might be the new Posh and Becks. Come on! We are talking about David Beckham here, and I am just some knacker doorman! They'd actually got a picture of Becks next to my mugshot that for the likes of me, is hysterical, a complete travesty. But you know what? Loads of celebrities actually keep these newspaper clippings of themselves. I think that's a bit weird. I don't give a shit – why keep them?

Click was an absolute golden period of my life. But as with so many things, change was round the corner. When I am feeling down I often think *What I wouldn't give just to have one of Click's good nights again?* A smile on everyone's faces before people started falling out, before it all went wrong; before all the arguments started, just looking at everyone happy, all my friends, smiles everywhere. I loved Click.

# CHAPTER FOURTEEN

# TEETERING ON THE ABYSS

Tash and me were living in Fulham when Josh arrived. It wasn't easy. We were both tired and not getting that much sleep. I was going off to work at Click; I used to scoot off at three in the morning in a car for late-night feeds then try to get some kip. Then Tash would be back at work doing TV or rehearsals or whatever. It was bloody hard work, but it's amazing how you cope: you don't care because it's your little baby. There's no one else who could piss on my face and get away with it!

When I think about the stuff I know about kids now and all the advice that is available, compared to what my parents had to go on when they were bringing us up, it's light years away. Fair play to me ma and da, I can't help but think how hard it was for them to provide food and shelter. How did they put up with me when I was a kid? And stuff like losing sight of him – we used to play out on the estate every night for hours. I couldn't see myself doing that with Josh. Once I lost sight of him in a shopping centre and the panic was all-consuming. In a second I went through panic, aggression, fear, more panic – it was awful. Then his little head popped up from behind a cartoon character's cardboard cut-out. He got a good telling-off for that, but only because it was so frightening and he needed to know not to wander off. We were born in a different time.

Josh is so like me when I was a kid. Everyone says he looks like me, for starters – he's got my best bits, my big toe and my little toe, and everything else is from Tash. One thing I will never waver from and that's making Josh feel good about himself. Unfortunately, I do feel that in this current day and age, from the second you are born some people are looking to bring you down and make you feel like shit. Sometimes Josh is naughty – of course, he's only a toddler – and a lot of the time he is very good, but no matter what, I will always support him. If the door opens when he is a young man and he comes in wearing a pink skirt, I'm not gonna expect it, but I will still tell him he's deadly.

It might surprise you to know that I believe in some form of reincarnation. I think that when you are born, they erase your memory and let you loose into the world again, afresh. I believe that people have been here before, there is some kind of loop. When I was young, my parents always said to me, 'There is an old soul in you, but they forgot to erase your memory.' Josh is the same. When he was only a few months old, we were on holiday in Gran Canaria with Tash's parents, having a cold beer. Josh starting crying and looking at the beer – it was really odd, almost like he'd recognised what it was. He was really squealing, so I dipped my finger in the suds of the beer and he licked it off and went, 'Ooohhh!'

He's way ahead of his years with the paparazzi, too. When he was very small, I think about six months old, Tash was coming out of a hotel with him in her arms and a bunch of paps jumped out and began flashing away at her, effectively in Josh's face. It totally freaked him out. Although he is only a toddler, he's learnt his lesson because when they start shooting pictures of us now, Josh will point his finger at them and, with a little frown on his face, say, 'No! You can't do that to me!'

He's always been into music. I used to have my decks in the kitchen – Tash used to hate that – and I'd feed him in his bouncer while I played some tunes and he'd be bouncing back and forth like mad! He loved it. He was on to birds from a very young age too. Sometimes he would come into the club's office if I had a meeting, and when the bar-girls walked by, Josh would lean forward and look after them as they passed! It was hilarious to see. He's just absolutely 100 per cent, a lovely kid. He has got a lot of good people around him too – there are so many people around Josh that love him.

The first time I took him to the zoo, he was really young. I don't think he was old enough to have much of a clue what he was looking at, to be honest but it was a nice day out, something different for him. We put him on this carousel and he absolutely loved it. So much so, in fact, that every time we went to get him off, he started bawling his eyes out. He ended up going around and around for ages. It got to the point where I began to get dizzy watching him, but he was still sitting there loving it. I recently bought him a massive toy jeep and was teaching him to drive it in the back garden; I always wanted one of those when I was a kid – they go fast and have gears and everything, so I got him one.

Josh was touring with his mom when he was only a few months old He's travelled more than most people do in their life: Asia, Europe, all over the gaff! When I was his age I was lucky if I went out of my garden.

Josh has got this fantastic aura about him, such a beautiful, mild manner. I just know he's going to do something in entertainment when he grows up, though, he's a proper born entertainer – he loves putting on a show; he gets that from his ma. And no matter what he does when he grows up, he will get enough information about it. If he comes to me and says, 'I want to start working on the door,' I will be like, 'OK, let me give you a few hints...' He will take his life the way he wants to, there's no point fighting it.

You suddenly have to watch your every move when you become a dad too, especially as I am on the telly sometimes and Josh might see it. In September 2005, I was doing some press interviews for the kids' channel, Nickelodeon, and this interviewer said to me, 'Can you burp for us?'

I said, 'What? Burp? Why?'

'Just burp into the camera.'

With only half a smile on my face, I said, 'You are exactly the type of person I tell my kid not to listen to.'

I still belched into the box for him, though.

It was such an incredible thing to become a father and, although it was tough, I loved every minute of it. So you can imagine how devastated Tash and me were, when Josh was just six months old, and the two of us decided to separate.

I'd been with Tash for nearly three years. At first, after I stopped working with Westlife and before Click opened, I was having quite a hard time because I hung around with Tash for a while so that we could spend more time together – after all, we'd spent months apart because of our respective jobs. The problem was, she was the only one really working full on, as I'd taken time off to go on the road with her. That felt very uncomfortable to me – I have to be doing something and contributing, making progress. Actually I went through a really dark time. I'd always been self-sufficient but now I began to depend on Tash for a living, which is not a good situation at all. It doesn't work.

Basically, it came to the point where we'd had a few fights over stupid shit. Tash wanted to make a career again; she'd been through a hard pregnancy and we had so much going on what with the band and Click. She wasn't really happy and neither was I, and even though we both knew we loved each other, it felt like one of us was going to have to bite the bullet. I rang her up and said, 'It's not working any more' and she was like, 'Yeah', so we agreed to go our separate ways.

It was hard, but we decided to separate and at least we didn't do it hating each other, or even not loving each other, it just wasn't working. At the end of the day it was the right decision at the time and we had discussed it in great depth. We were better off separated than being unhappy with each other.

I rang up a mate and said, 'I need somewhere to stay.' 'Are you sure about this, Fran?' he asked. But I was. I went down and stayed at his gaff on the couch. Tash was doing a gig so I went back the next morning while she was out. I didn't take anything that was 'ours', the computer and other shit like that. I left pretty much everything. All I took was my clothes.

Tash's mom and dad had been helping us by looking after Josh in the week because I was working nights and Tash was working very hard travelling too; it was impossible for us at times. I was absolutely devastated when we split, I felt like a complete failure. I'd got a kid and now I was not with him. I'll be honest with you, it makes me feel upset writing this. When we separated, I used to ring Tash's mom and dad every single day to speak to Josh. Even though he was a tiny kid, they used to put the phone to his ear and he'd be on the line for ages listening to my voice. I saw him whenever I could – initially he was in Liverpool and I used to drive up there and see him, then drive straight back. I did whatever it took to spend time with him.

Me and Tash always got on well and made sure that as far as Josh was concerned it was all cool. There was a bit of friction in the first few weeks, but anyone who has gone through a hard break-up will know that if you really care for someone, you feel immense pain. It's a pain you can't describe, a sick feeling; you're completely twisted inside, there is something missing. I can't speak for Tash, but the pain I was feeling at the start was shockingly intense – this was someone I spoke to or saw every day, then all of a sudden, nothing; I'd moved out and that connection was broken. Except my pain was doubled because of Josh.

I saw Josh all the time and once me and Tash got through those hard first few weeks, we said to each other, 'This is all about Josh and that has to be the priority.' I honestly feel that Josh never knew any different. He would come to stay with me, I would go and see him, Tash would ring me up whenever she wanted and we settled into a nice routine of just getting on with it. You keep it regular, so he had a foundation in his life that he could understand.

One week after I broke up with Tash, a tabloid

newspaper called me up and said they wanted to do an interview about Click and all the stuff going on. I went to the offices and sat down, then noticed this large laundry bag at the side of the table. They placed it on the top of the table, open right in front of me so I could see all the wads of money inside (it turned out to be £26,000) and said, 'Tell us dirt.'

I asked, 'What are you talking about?' They said, 'Here's the deal, we have a laundry bag full of cash, you take it and dish the dirt on Atomic Kitten, any in-fighting, all that stuff.' I called their bluff, put my fingers round the bag's handles and said, 'OK, lads, no problem,' and their eyes lit up, but I was only joking of course. Then, I stood up and, with the bag in my hand, said, 'I love Natasha, I love my son, I think the Kittens are lovely and I like the other girls and all that I have to say is that I am gonna miss them all. Thanks very much, see you later,' and made to walk out of the office with the money.

I stopped at the door, though, and turned round to face them again. I had no issue with them, this was their job, after all, but I felt like explaining myself a bit further: 'I would never shit on my friends. Never! I will live in a box on Oxford Street, climbing in and out singing Westlife songs, before I will ever say a bad word about any of them. So thanks, but no thanks.' I left the cash and, as I was walking out the door, one of the guys came after me, caught up with me by the lift and said, 'You are one of the first people who's said no to money like that. Fair play to you.' He also said, 'If you've ever got any problems, give us a shout. I have a lot of respect for you for doing that.'

I needed to start afresh, so I got a place in Maida Vale. I used to love it when Josh came to stay over with me for two days there. It was the only night of the week I used to get into bed at 8pm. I would crawl under the sheets and put my arm around him; despite all the heartache and all the craziness happening in my life, at that precise moment I was actually a happy man, truly happy.

When Tash started a relationship with a new man called Gavin Hatcher, it was very tough for me. As her ex-partner, all I ever wanted was for her to be happy, there was no bitterness or desire to see her new relationship fail. I always loved her, so I wanted her to be happy. But with regard to Josh, it was extremely difficult. After all, it meant that another man would see my son more than I would. Gavin was a nice lad and Tash had picked someone she wanted to be with, so I trusted her that he wasn't going to be a wanker. But I can't deny it was weird.

As it goes, I suppose I was the worst ex-boyfriend in the world – dropping Josh off in this huge Voyager people carrier. However, I was always polite, humble and went out of my way to stay out of any confrontation if I possibly could. That said, the very first time I dropped Josh off to Gavin... oh, Jesus, Josh started crying and he gave me a hug and didn't want me to go. It was incredibly painful, awful. I took a deep breath, said, 'See you later,' and walked off round the corner. I was not a happy man. I can honestly say I have never had that feeling before in my life, and I wouldn't wish it on anyone, it was emotional hell. But I knew these were the parameters that had been set now and, for Josh's sake, I had to fit in around the new rules.

Unfortunately, fitting in like that came at a price. My mates had said to prepare myself for what would be a difficult time when I first started visiting Josh. I'll be honest with you – I disguised my feelings. I was hurting something terrible. I had never been so immersed in the madness of clubland – on the one hand, I had got to be the party animal every night and yet every day I was living through darkness. I veered off into all sorts of things to try to hide the hurt that was chewing me up inside. And I often found solace at the bottom of a bottle.

Pretty soon, I ended up shutting myself off from everything for a while; I climbed into this misty bubble and closed myself off from everyone and everything. I was running on auto-pilot, I think that was the only way I could deal with what I was going through back then. You see, I'd always said that no matter what I did in life, I would never ever have my kid grow up without me, and yet that's exactly what had happened.

There were so many dark moments for me back then. It was undoubtedly the hardest time of my life. One night I walked into my club at midnight and sat down, had a few drinks; people were coming over and saying 'hello' and I was being the friendly club host as usual. I

*Top*: The line-up of *I'm A Celebrity, Get Me Out Of Here!*

*Bottom*: Paul Burrell, Joe Pasquale and me.

This was on set at the 118888 TV advert I did.

Me at the film audition – when I was at my biggest ever!

*Inset*: my official 'door supervisor' clearance from Westminster Council.

Out at Trap with Kelli Young, my ex who was in Liberty X.

t the launch of a website with Ronan Keating in October 2005.

Paul and me.

My son Josh and me backstage at 02 In The Park in Dublin in 2005.

The photographers finally managed to catch me and Tash together after we came out of club in August 2005 and then everyone knew it was back on again between the two of us

was wearing sunglasses, though. It looked strange in a club but I just felt I needed to hide behind them. There I was, sitting in my own central London nightclub, champagne flowing, beautiful women everywhere, friends partying next to me and yet all I could think about was what I would have given to be at home in bed with Tash and Josh.

In life it's sometimes very easy to hide yourself behind the booze. Even though I was working and doing my thing, I simply wasn't able to deal with what was happening, I just tried to blank it out. I was utterly miserable, while at the same time I was being paid to make everyone else happy.

# CHAPTER FIFTEEN

# THE TRAIN WON'T STOP

Fortunately, this emotional black hole only took hold of me for a few weeks. Then, one morning, I woke up and said, 'Enough, I am going to find a way through this.' I will always eventually find out how to get through a situation, no matter how hard it may seem at the time, and I realised this was just one more thing I had to get through. I was nervous – I didn't know how I would get through it, but I was damn well going to try. I said to myself that no matter what happened, I would find a way to get over it – and I did.

It was a long time after I split up with Tash before I saw anyone else. From the minute we separated, I never got over her and never stopped thinking about her, even though I did spend time with other women. One person most people know I dated for a while is Jodie Marsh. This is the blunt reality about myself and Jodie Marsh: we met each other, we became really close friends but we should have stayed friends. Unfortunately we didn't, the relationship didn't work out and I wish her all the best.

There are those who are quick to talk London down and say it is full of rude people and its sheer pace stamps on your life. From my experience, that couldn't be further from the truth. Sure, there are people you encounter who could do with a few lessons in manners, but it is a major capital city with millions of inhabitants crammed in there, so you will always get that. For my part, I have to say that since arriving in London I have met some of the most amazing friends you could wish for, proper friends who would do anything for you.

I grew up when I moved to London. I found things in myself I never knew I had. London showed me that I can get through anything, I have that ability, no matter how low I get. And as for extinguishing people's dreams because London life is tough – come on! I started off living in what amounted to little more than a squat, penniless, but then London gave me a security badge and a job at Home, high-profile door work, a world tour with a pop band, my own clubs, the love of my life... the list is endless.

Take Rachel, my best friend. I met her in Home when she was working on the VIP door. We got on like a house on fire and we've been best friends ever since. When I met her she was dead opinionated, looked totally cool and I quickly came to love her like a sister. Rachel is my conscience – every time I look like I'm getting in trouble, she will push her hand into the bubble and pull me out. She keeps me on the straight and narrow... for a little while, anyway! She was a top door bird too, always looking after me. The first time I met Rachel's mom, me and Calum Best had been on the piss for about four days and we were sitting in the VIP bar in Click on the back of the chairs with countless bottles of booze spread out on the table. When Rachel came in to introduce her mom, I told her that her daughter was one of the nicest people I'd ever met and that she'd done one of the best jobs bringing her up.

Another fantastic mate I've met because of living and working in London is Adee Phelan. I was walking down Wardour Street one day when I saw Adee and said, 'All right, what's the story?' We were chatting away and saw each other around a few times then gradually he started hanging out at the club. One night I saw him in there with a few mutual friends so I said, 'Come on over and have a drink!' He sat down with me and we had an absolutely riotous laugh, we just got on so well straight away.

He was doing the TV show called *The Salon* at the time, set in the hair studio he ran with his partner Paul. It was a really popular 'reality' show but for Adee it meant very long working days. Plus, he was on camera all the time and being watched by millions of people, so this was one very busy period for him. Meeting me was the beginning of the end for Adee.

Within a few months of hanging around with me, they thought Adee had a brain tumour and was going to die, he was so ill! We partied so hard, every night. I used to pick him up at 11pm and party all night then we'd drop him off for *The Salon* at 7am. While we all went off home to get some kip, Adee would have a full twelve-hour shift ahead of him, at the end of which I would be waiting outside in my car for the next night out. Sometimes he seemed to go for days without getting any sleep. We had some of the best nights ever though; we've always had a ball.

One night we were sitting in a club having a late drink and I noticed Adee wasn't around. Next thing I know he came back to the table and said, 'This bloke just punched me in the head on the stairs!' We ran around the club trying to find him but to no avail, so we sat Adee down and poured him four shots. He'd already got this massive bruise swelling up on his face and said he couldn't feel anything because it was numb.

I asked him what the fight had been about and he told me this guy had called him 'a gay hairdresser', which obviously he isn't. Then Adee told me, 'I wanted to have a go and I've been hanging round with you so much I thought it would have rubbed off on me a bit... but it didn't.' He was trying to act tough and got smacked; we were laughing so much over that one.

We sat drinking until the early morning but the next day he was filming *The Salon* so we dropped him off. Me and all the lads headed back to my gaff. It was hilarious because we switched the telly on and there was Adee, live on national TV, obviously hung-over and with this great big black eye. He put a pair of huge shades on to try and hide it; we were in tears laughing.

For Christmas 2004, me and Adee went to Marbella and had the time of our life. You know those 'Lucky-Lucky!' blokes who come round trying to sell you watches, glasses, sandals, wristbands or whatever? Normally they have to work really hard just to get one sale. Well, me and Adee tried to buy as much stuff off them as we could afford, just for the craic. We started off buying about twenty pairs of sunglasses with wipers on the front of them and we were doing this little Irish jig in the pub wearing these bloody things. Then another lucky-lucky guy walks in with a case full of watches, about eighty of them, which were about twenty euros each. I asked, 'How much for all the watches?'

He said, 'What? All the watches?'

'Yes, every one, how much?'

'One thousand euros.'

'Mate, no way, all I've got is 700 euros – you can have that for all the watches.'

He nearly took my hand off grabbing the money!

We spent the rest of the night handing them out to the kids in the pub and having a right laugh. Every time a lucky-lucky man came in selling watches, we'd say, 'How much are you charging? We are only asking for a fiver!' It was a scream. We ended up having so much to drink the hotel owner wouldn't let us in. Me da was bursting to go to the toilet but then he slipped over and I was on the ground in stitches, pissing myself laughing, saying, 'Look at me old man, he's desperate for the toilet!' but this hotel owner was not having it, he was going, 'No! You are crazy people, you can't come in.' Me and Adee have never laughed so much. Adee is a classic mate; I love him to bits.

That's the sort of person London has introduced to me. As I have said, I always felt a draw to London, even when I was a kid growing up on the estate near Dublin but the reality of actually coming here to live and work had been far, far better. And there was more to come...

By now, I was very well known around London's clubland so perhaps it wasn't surprising when I was approached by some businessmen who wanted to open up a new celebrity nightclub. Without blowing my own trumpet, by this point I could bring a lot of stuff to the table and people knew that.

Click was massive, don't get me wrong, but I was listening to a few people who wanted to do a bigger project. To be frank, with the benefit of hindsight I wish I could go back and listen to what my head was telling me at the time, which was to say 'No!' I was at a stage when my life was just mad, though, and I missed Tash terribly through that whole period. I had never got over her, nowhere near. Life just wasn't the same without her. Maybe the new club was a way of me attempting to find a new focus, I don't know.

We bought the building that housed what would be called Trap nightclub, on Wardour Street, just off Oxford Street; it was a very old club in need of some updating. I have always been pretty swift at sorting out a club's premises, just like back in the days of Leeson Street,

Dublin, and this was no exception. I think we turned it around into being ready to open as a VIP club in just over two days. For me, Trap was all about the next big phase, moving onward and upward. I always have to have my foot to the floor otherwise I feel stagnant and become down. Click had been the most famous celebrity club in town, but that wasn't enough for me at the time.

When I left Click, everyone came with me to Trap – the party simply moved on. Looking back, I have many good memories of Trap too. Pharrell Williams came in one night, jumped up on these leather couches and started doing all these dance moves. Suddenly loads of girls jumped up there too in their heels and began dancing around him. My security guys looked to me to get them all down but I said, 'You can't, there's too many of them... and besides, they're having a great time!' There's always that balance you have to strike when a celebrity is in your club. When the lights went up at the end of the night after the club was closed, it became apparent that these leather couches were peppered with holes from the heels – they were destroyed! I phoned the repair man the next day and he said it was going to cost £4,000! Argh! Busta Rhymes came down one night with about forty people and took the whole back section over. I was like, *Wicked! We will take loads of money tonight.* He was really cool, came over and asked, 'What about some food, you got anything we can eat?' so I closed the whole upstairs restaurant down for him and all his mates to make sure they had a great time. We had all sorts of amazing dishes on the menu but do you know what they ordered? Fifty plates of fish and chips! I kid you not, it was 5am and they wanted fifty fish and chips.

The chef was like, 'What?' So I got on the phone to various mates, saying 'Does anyone know where we can get fish and chips right now?' By chance, there was a late-night fish-and-chip shop just down the road so I ran down there, crashed in and asked, 'Can you do me some food straight away?' Between this chip shop and my place we just about had the capacity to sort the order. I spent about forty minutes running up and down the street juggling about eight plates of fish and chips at a time, sweating like a pig, then strolling into the restaurant, calm as you like, serving up the dishes. I got it done in the end – it was mad, though.

One thing I relish about owning a nightclub is the opportunity it gives you to make a difference to normal people every night of the week, to make a particular night the best night of their lives. One evening, a couple of really good-looking black guys showed up: you could tell they went to the gym, they dressed well and had great physiques. Their mate came too – he was really quite overweight and less striking, but I really liked him, he had a personality the size of the world. They came the next night too and soon became regulars.

This bigger lad always told me how much he wanted to get into the VIP room. One night I was dancing on the bass bins in my club, as you do, and this kid came over to me and asked, 'Can you get me in the VIP room?' I went,

'No, mate, listen, it's not that simple tonight...' As I was talking to him, one of his good-looking mates turned around and went 'Tssk!' in my direction.

I looked at him and I thought, *Mate, I am going to prove something to you.* So I took hold of the big fella, got him two bottles of champagne and brought him to my personal table in the VIP room, which was always rammed with a load of glamour girls. I said to two of these girls, 'Can you do me a favour? This guy is a friend of mine, go outside and put your hands around him and make him feel special.' They did the whole thing with him with champagne, went outside, partied, met all his mates and he went home with the biggest smile on his face you ever saw. What's more, he ended up dating one of those glamour girls for about six months! To this day, when I bump into him every now and again, he is always very kind and says, 'You changed my life.' Owning a club allows me to do things like that for people, and I'm not lying when I say I really enjoy that aspect of it.

I was partying really hard at this point too. I had met Kelli Young from Liberty X and we had started going out. I'd seen her and the rest of the group around at gigs and that, but we'd never really spoken before. One night I was with Adee in Click drinking bottles of champagne around my table, when someone slapped me on the back and I spurted out this bubbly all across the table. Kelli was sitting opposite with some friends and it went all over her. I was so embarrassed, it was pretty much the first time I'd had a one-to-one conversation with her and it was to apologise for drenching her with champagne. She was really cool about it, though, and we spent most of that night having a chat and a laugh. She seemed different to all the other birds around; she wasn't into the scene and the whole partying side of the business.

We saw each other a few times in the next few weeks, really got on well and eventually began going out together. It's funny because from the second I met her, she was always trying to break it off with me! She was very quiet, just the opposite of me really, so it was an unusual mix. One time she was working in Ireland and we were enjoying our breakfast when I opened the papers and there was a picture of her and Colin Farrell, with a caption saying they were together! Laughing, I asked, 'Were you with Colin the other night, then?' and she just said, 'What? No!' I started winding her up about it, telling her, 'At least he's Irish!'

Despite the two of us being so different, we got on really well, I thought Kelli was a really cool bird. She is a dead sound girl, and even after we broke up we remained great friends. I do not have a bad word to say about her. It was a shame, really, because when I was with Kelli, I wasn't really in a good place to be with someone – my life was just mental. Partying all night, sleeping all day, then getting picked up in a car packed with lads, then starting all over again seven days a week. I was so embroiled in the image of 'doing the London thing'. The madder we were, the crazier we were the better – or so it seemed to me at the time. The pace of my life was insane.

The problem was, Trap also became very successful very quickly and this time the amount of business meetings, demands and organisation was massive. There were hooks pulling at me from every angle, I was starting to get really confused, people wanting all sorts all the time, people wanting a say here and there. Trap started off tremendously, but sustaining any club is difficult. It became over-popular, too big, too quick, and began causing a lot of turmoil in my life. Add this to my exhausting party lifestyle and I was just becoming a shell. I found myself going to the cinema in the day on my own a lot – I would switch off the phone and just get some peace for an hour or two, escaping into the silver screen. (I still love to do that!) But I knew deep down I wasn't confronting the issues that were buzzing around my head like vultures.

There were so many successes and I knew inside that I had already – before Trap even – done the 'club' dream to a point way beyond anything anyone would have expected of me. Yet despite this, I started to feel a need, a drag to do something new, to get a fresh buzz; I wasn't getting the same satisfaction out of the business. I hope that doesn't sound ungrateful – believe me, I know exactly how lucky I was and I also know how hard I grafted and how many risks I had taken. It was just that my inner psyche was craving for more again.

I am always scared to take my foot off the pedal – friends often say, 'Give yourself some credit.' I know my days in school affected me in this respect, especially being told I would never achieve anything and sitting at the back in all the lower classes. But as an adult, that focus and drive has always been there, it's never dimmed. I don't know what I am trying to prove to myself; maybe I never will. I am a perfectionist and my own harshest critic. If I fail or let someone down, I beat myself up badly and for a long time. I can sit there for hours chastising myself. I know I do it and I know this creates a lot of pressure on myself to keep succeeding, achieving, moving forward, but that's just the way I am. I don't see how I can change that, and I think that probably without that inner drive I wouldn't have achieved what I have.

I began to feel down and the more successful Trap became, the more it seemed to fester. I hit a low point when I thought, *What is my next step?* This had been my perfect dream for the whole of my life; since I was a kid I wanted to own clubs. I had achieved many things but I still hadn't proved enough to myself. I couldn't take my foot off the pedal. Here I was, 26 years old, owning *the* VIP club in London.

I'd done it... and yet I wanted more.

# CHAPTER SIXTEEN

# JUNGLE AND ORGIES

I am a massive fan of Michael Moore. I've always loved documentary-style films, as well as feature films, and he's one of the most controversial and talented in this genre. When I saw Moore's first movie, *Roger & Me*, it was the first time I'd seen a feature-length documentary done like that and for me, it was reality. He's a normal motherfucker with a camera! I had read all about *Fahrenheit 911* well in advance and was really looking forward to seeing it. So much so, in fact, that I found out the time and place of the very first UK public screening, which was in Leicester Square at about 11.30 in the morning.

When I arrived in the West End, there were only about fifteen or so people ahead of me in the queue, but within a short while the line had swollen to over a hundred die-hard Moore fans. Right in front of me in the queue were two men who I can only describe as looking like professors – corduroy trousers, briefcases with thin, wiry hair. I didn't care what they looked like or what they did because we were all obviously fans of the same man, or at least keen to see his new work. I was wearing a baseball cap sideways with some really baggy shorts and a T-shirt. One of the professors turned around, looked me up and down and then tutted loudly, 'Tsssk!'

I'm not sure what he was thinking. Surely it was obvious that you don't go to see a film like *Fahrenheit 911* at that time in the morning unless you are clued up about what's going on and what will be in it? I just nodded my head slowly, then lifted my hands up in the air and shouted at the top of my voice, 'Excuse me everybody, is this the queue for *Shrek 2?*'

I was laughing but at the same time I was disgusted by the attitudes of these 'professors'. Everyone around us giggled and I had made my point, but I wanted to have a word in private too. 'Don't judge a book by its cover! I know why I'm here. Why are you here?' The man just turned back round clutching his briefcase tightly and said nothing.

In the aftermath of various stories in the papers and the series of events at Trap, a lot of people felt they could easily judge my book by its cover. Unbeknown to me, a chance meeting was about to send me halfway around the world into a jungle campsite that would give me the opportunity to show people who I really was, and not just fuel some preconception they had about me. I was about to experience a twist of fate that would change my life forever.

A lot of people ask me how I came to be in the Australian jungle in January 2004 for the fourth series of *I'm A Celebrity... Get Me Out Of Here!* I've got to be honest: I often ask myself the same question. How it all came about is... well, the only word for it is jammy! I was at a TV studio – I can't recall if it was with Tash or Westlife because I've had to go to studios so many times. As I was walking along this long corridor, I accidentally bumped into this lady. I apologised profusely but we started chatting and got on really well. Then I went on my way and thought nothing more of it.

It turns out this lady was one of the heads of programming at ITV.

So imagine my surprise when, over two months later, I took a phone call from my agent James Spallone saying they wanted me to do *I'm A Celebrity... Get Me Out Of Here!* My first reaction was to think, *But I'm not a celebrity!* It seemed this lady thought I would make a very interesting addition to the line-up. I know I have mentioned manners and being polite a few times, but I do firmly believe that in life, if you treat everyone the way you want to be treated, good things will come your way. I could have just ignored that lady I bumped into or said a quick sorry and rushed past, but I'd never do that, I was always going to stop and apologise properly, make sure she was OK. It's just common courtesy.

When I first came to London, I worked so hard on doors getting to know people. I just used to say to myself, *Every single person I meet could be the one person who helps me, who opens a door for me.* That's why working the doors was the best job because all day long I met people. Working doors and VIP bars I got to know hundreds of celebrities, TV producers, actors, agents, good guys, bad guys, people from all walks of life. And, as I've said, you can make these people have the very best night of their lives very easily, by treating them nice, by treating them the way you would like to be treated. That's what I had done that day when I bumped into that lady in that corridor. Suddenly, this latest door had been opened.

When James called me and told me I'd been invited on, I said, 'No way!' because I just thought he was pulling my leg. Kerry Katona had just won the previous series so I knew all about the show and what it could mean in terms of your career. Once when I was in Jodie's gaff watching Peter Andre, we'd chatted about the programme and I'd said to myself, *I don't think I could do that.* However, as surprised as I was to be asked, at that time in my life it was not an avenue I could see myself going down. I pointed out I was not a celebrity and that I didn't want to open myself up to that world. I was a nightclub owner, I knew everyone around town, I worked very hard but I certainly wasn't a celebrity. Plus, I'd never wanted to do TV, and perhaps there was an element of me not being sure if I had the balls to do it. So I thanked ITV for their interest and then said 'No.'

In my life, if I believe in something that's how I make decisions. This was a situation where every instinct in my body told me to decline, so I did. At this point they went away and someone else was approached, but in the last few days there were problems agreeing terms, apparently. Eventually, I understand, the plug was pulled because no agreement could be made.

Meantime, I had seen the publicity and hype for the forthcoming show and I must admit, I had started to wonder if I'd made the right decision after all to decline the offer. I spoke with James and made it clear that maybe we should have said yes, and that if we were called again, we should accept the offer. The problem was, this was such a popular show and so many celebs were keen to go on, it was unlikely I'd get a second chance.

To compound the problems, my life was very complicated at this time. There'd been stuff in the papers – not by Jodie, I might add – about my business and the club was proving to be very stressful indeed. Overnight I went from being popular with everybody to walking into my local shop and finding everyone looking at me suspiciously. It was a bad time. I was so down and depressed, about business and life and just everything. I still missed Tash desperately. And I was bored out of my mind with certain aspects of my life.

Trap was proving to be a great club, but I was really miserable and I look back on that period as a very dark phase. It was a hard year. I had come to a stagnant point in my life where everything I had been working for had been taken as far as I thought it could go and the only way I could see it progressing was by starting to come down, to lose momentum. I am the type of person who needs to be moving forward, but with the situation I was in, I could see no prospect of that in the near future.

I was walking down Oxford Street one day and happened to take a phone call that was just pure, absolute stress. I won't go into details but suffice to say it was a big argument with someone that was getting out of hand. I had been physically attacked and had defended myself, but the repercussions were continuing for weeks, this person just wouldn't let it go. There'd been a fight in the club and unlike most fights where it's finished that night, this altercation led to people being pissed off for some time, which festered into an on-going rift that was causing a lot of stress. It was really stressful, let me tell you.

I got off that call and I was really vexed. Then the phone rang again almost immediately. It said, 'James' so I took the call.

'Hey, Fran? It's James, listen. Pack your bags, you're going to the jungle!'

Where I had been apprehensive before and eventually said no, this time I actually clenched my fist, punched the air in the middle of the street and shouted, 'Yes!'

Just prior to going to the jungle, I'd got so down that I'd withdrawn from most of my friends and the clubland lifestyle that had been a central part of my life for years. I just felt I needed to take a step back, look at myself again and find some sense in all the madness. So I pulled away from Trap and a lot of my mates, bought a place in the Docklands miles away from anywhere and spent almost all of my time there. I was cocooned in that flat, watching movies, eating food, not going out, spending time with my kid, just keeping myself to myself. Apart from the days I was with Josh, I felt awful.

After a while, some friends took me to one side and said they were worried about me but I told them there was no need. I just needed to reassess my life, find out what was the next stage for me. And through the madness of it all, along comes the jungle like a white horse running into a burning field of flames. That's the only way I can describe it: that jungle experience brought back something into my life that had been extinguished. At that point in my life, I couldn't do it any more, I didn't want to; I needed change.

No matter how low I get, and how hard things become, I have the ability to pick myself up somehow. I have to keep going. Yet sometimes you need a little slice of luck to give yourself the environment in which to make that next leap forward. One day, when I was feeling particularly low, Kelli from Liberty X had said to me, 'You know what? I don't know how or why, but something always happens for you. It will again this time, you'll see.' And here I was, literally just in the nick of time, flying into the jungle. My whole life has been like that – just when I really need something to come along and pick me up and take me on another unknown expedition, something always happens. This time, I had nothing to lose.

As I pressed the 'end call' button after speaking to James, I was like 'I'm out of here!' In the aftermath of certain things that had been said about me in the papers, this was also a unique opportunity to speak up for myself in the purest way – by just being me. Go out there, be myself and see what happens. It was certainly a great chance to put right so many of the bad things that had been said about me and show people who I really was.

Of course, I'd never done anything like it before and this particular show had such a high profile. I wasn't scared, though, I just said to myself, *Take this one day at a time.* I had nothing to prove to anyone, and unlike a lot of people who go there to revive careers and get media exposure I didn't need to do that. All I had to do was be myself. The worst-case scenario was that I went in for two or three days, got kicked out first, then went jet-skiing with me mates for three weeks.

Next thing I know, I'm doing photo shoots and meetings and being sent information about my flight out. Before I'd had chance to collect myself, I was waiting with a brand-new suitcase for my taxi to Heathrow. I was on my way to the Australian jungle! The car that ITV sent to pick me up was a dodgy cab. At one point the driver actually asked me if I would like to drive! I had to direct this nutcase to Heathrow. Mental! When I got out at the airport and found the lady from ITV, the first thing I asked her was, 'Where did you get that cab from?' It was a mad start to an insane few weeks.

Things got rapidly worse, though! I went to the counter to get my tickets and paperwork and the women there said my visa was not stamped and so I could not fly.

I couldn't believe it, what a start. I said, 'Come on, ladies, you gotta help me here, please!' Then one of them said, 'If you sing me a song, I will stamp your visa.'

'What? Did I hear you correctly?'

'Yes, sing me a song, in fact a Westlife song, and I will stamp your visa.'

'Oh, you gotta be kidding me? A Westlife song as well?'

Well, I felt like a right tit standing in Heathrow singing a Westlife song, but I really wanted to go to the jungle and it got my visa stamped. I can't even remember what it was I sang now, but it was probably 'Flying Without Wings' or 'Uptown Girl'.

I got on the plane, found the lady from ITV and she said, 'I've already heard two or three stories about you and we are not out there yet!' She was funny; we got on really well, a nice bird. I was sitting in first class and all these posh people were looking at me; the expressions on their faces were clearly saying, *Why are you here?* I sat back in that luxurious leather recliner and the expression on my face said *It's none of your business!*

We had a connecting flight that stopped at Singapore and for most of the flight I put Atomic Kitten on in my headphones – it's sad, but I did. When Josh was going to bed, I always used to play a couple of Kittens songs, so I was very emotional hearing that, 35,000 feet up, flying so many miles away from him for weeks. It was a brutal flight.

When I landed, I walked out of the airport and all the paps were there and they were saying, 'Fair play to you,

Fran, for getting out here!' 'God knows how I did, to be honest with you,' I told them. And they said, 'Well, there were a lot of people trying to get out here, but you did, so fair play!' They've always been so good to me, they really have.

I was assigned a chaperone in Australia because at this point we were still not allowed to know who else was going on the show and we certainly weren't allowed to meet them. My chaperone introduced herself, then turned to me and said,

'Can I ask you a question?'

'Yes, of course, what can I do for you?' I replied.

'Who the fuck are you?'

The only answer I could honestly say was, 'Fucking nobody!'

'So how did you get this programme?'

'As I sit in the back of this car with you, on my way into the jungle in a couple of days, I actually genuinely don't have a clue.'

I explained to her that I own and run nightclubs, DJ sometimes and do this and that, but that essentially I didn't know how or why either. She thought Kylie's ex-boyfriend James Gooding was coming but was glad it wasn't him because out in Oz, Kylie is obviously their princess.

We pulled up at the hotel, I checked in and was looking forward to crashing out in my room. Before I could though, the woman from ITV told me I had been assigned a bodyguard. A bodyguard!

'I don't want a bodyguard! What do I want one for?'

'Everyone's got one, Fran.'

The irony of being allocated a bodyguard wasn't lost on me, let me tell you.

This bodyguard came over and said, 'Hello, I've been warned about you, I know what you used to do.'

'I'm not going to cause you any problems, mate,' I said, with a smile on my face, 'This will be a piece of piss.'

We headed into the lift and up to my room, where I flung my brand-new suitcase onto the bed and tried to open it. But it was locked and I couldn't find the key. I looked across at the bodyguard and said, 'Pass me that knife, please.' He threw the knife over and I stabbed it into the top of the case, then peeled the lid back like a tin of meat, pulled my clothes out and threw the case to one side. 'Sorted! Don't worry about it, you've only got me for three days!'

I was only at the hotel for three days before I went into the jungle, but I got on very well with that bodyguard. At one point he told me, 'You are not allowed out for these three days at all, because they don't want any contestants bumping into each another... and they don't want you getting into trouble.'

'What? I'm not allowed to go into town? For three days? Are you joking?'

'That's my instructions, yes.'

I wasn't about to cause trouble (yet), so I said, 'Fair enough' and went and sat on my bed. The bodyguard stood outside my hotel room in the corridor, on guard if you like. I waited a few minutes then popped my head out of my door and said, 'At least come and sit in here with me.' He came in and sat down on a chair, and I went into my bedroom and shut the door. I opened the window, scaled down the drainpipe from my second-storey room, jumped to the ground, ran back into reception, called the lift, went up to the second floor, walked to my room and knocked on the door. When my bodyguard opened the door to find me standing outside smiling at him I said, 'Look, mate, if I want to go out, I'm going out, so you might as well come with me!'

He graciously admitted defeat and agreed to come out on the town with me. We got a few people together and had a mental night. It was a good time to be partying, because it was what they call 'Schooly Week' over there, when everyone who has left school basically goes out and gets mashed for days on end. We went rolling from gaff to gaff, drinking and having a great time.

Along the way, we bumped into another bodyguard and got chatting and he inadvertently paid me a very nice compliment. He said, 'Do you know who you remind me of? I worked this show last year and you are just like John Lydon. I spent a lot of time with John and I'm telling you, the way you talk and your views on life, the way you think about things, you are very similar!' I was really pleased to hear that.

Towards the end of the night, this stunning bird came up and started talking to me. After a while she said, 'Can I come back?' So we started heading back to my hotel

and then she said, 'Can I bring my sister?' I said, 'What?'
So she goes and gets her sister and I was like, 'Oh, my
God!' We carried on walking and then these two gay
blokes were walking up the road and they said, 'We are
coming too!' then another bloke joined the line, it was
bizarre, I felt like the bloody Pied Piper! By the end of
that day I knew all the local doormen and could have got
into any club. My first night out in Oz and I mashed the
gaff! The next morning at 10am, I had to meet the
show's doctor and do all these check-ups and the
resident psychologist's verdict on me was that I was 'a
mentaller'. Yes!

After that, one of the producers came into my room,
sat down and asked me, 'Would you jump out of a
plane?' And I said, 'OK.' Then she asked me to sign a
form – the 'parachute' form, basically – to that effect.
'But we are not saying it will be you, Fran, just checking.'
Yeah, right!

That night I went for a meal and my phone was
ringing off the hook with people wishing me well and
telling me, 'Mate, you are going to be in there until the
end!' After the meal, I went back to the hotel, got some
sleep, woke up the next morning, went to the gym, got
picked up, gave them my bags, then joined this
procession of cars heading off for the start of the show.

We were sitting alone in these cars in a row with all
these security men standing by the windows. I was bored
off my tits, so I buzzed down the window, lunged out at
the bodyguard and pulled him back against the car,

desperately trying to drag him in. All the other bodyguards came running over and they were scraping me off him and I was crying with laughter, it was such a funny time. You see, the other contestants later told me they found this wait in the car extremely stressful and unsettling. They all went mad, but for me I couldn't help but sit there looking at the security thinking, *That's me standing out in the road, what am I doing sitting in the car?* It felt so strange to be on the other side of the fence.

Then they filmed you getting out of your car, but I had to do it six times to get it right. All the paps were laughing at me, and I was saying, 'Lads, give me a break – I am not exactly a professional!' The first person to come in behind me was Joe Pasquale. Everyone said to me the first people out would be Joe, Paul and myself but it turned out we were the three finalists.

We all met up and Joe said 'Hi', so did Paul. The model Sophie Anderton was going in too and the papers had been building up this intrigue about the likelihood of me trying it on with her. Well, her boyfriend was there, he owns a club down the road from mine and he's a friend, so I told them, 'Before you say anything, I never said a word!' and they were cool, they know what the papers can be like. While we were all chatting away, I was looking around the room, thinking what an odd one out I was.

I was asking everyone if they had signed the parachute form and only half had done so. Finally we were on our way but separated into groups, using the names 'Air',

'Fire' and 'Water'. When they said myself, Joe Pasquale and Paul Burrell were 'Air', I turned around to them – knowing they had both signed the parachute form – and told them, 'We are so jumping out of an aeroplane, I am telling you!' What a way to enter a programme, half an hour in and you're jumping out of a plane. I was right: of course we were the 'fall guys'!

I'd never met Paul or Joe before, yet suddenly, here we were, a trio of intrepid, albeit slightly nervous adventurers climbing through the clouds with the sole purpose of getting as high as possible before jumping back down to earth again. I have to tell you, it felt *fantastic*!

I knew Joe and Paul struggled with their nerves – it was a 14,000-feet free-fall, after all, not something to be taken lightly. But, for my part, I just had this powerful surge of excitement, adrenalin, energy, call it what you will. As I said at the very start of this book, it was tangibly a life-changing moment. I could feel my world altering with every minute that we climbed into the sky. It was just the most incredible experience.

Then it came time to jump out and I was pulling at the leash to go first. When I fell off the side of that plane and was plummeting through the clouds, the clarity of my thoughts was just amazing. In one sense, I'd never been so isolated, and with that came an overwhelming sense of wellbeing, of perspective. I vividly remember thinking *Nothing will ever vex me again.* When my feet touched down on the jungle earth just over a minute later, I was a changed man.

My first impressions when I got into the jungle site were how basic it was and how much hard work we had ahead of us. They have a few people scattered around the outskirts of the camp to stop the really dangerous creatures getting in – no one wants I'm A Dead Celebrity... Get Me Out Of Here! – but apart from that, it is all very real.

Matters were made worse for me because for the first week or so I didn't even have a proper bed. When we got there, we were a bed short and one person was going to end up on this most basic of hammocks slung between two trees. I knew straight away this would be a test of each individual's team spirit: *I'll see who sets themselves out for the best bed*, I thought to myself; *if someone is not going to get a bed, why not let it be me?* I'll tell you why not: I didn't sleep a night during the first week. It was impossible to kip in that thing, so I ended up just sitting all through the night by the fire. I looked rough; it was a nightmare. I started feeling really weak and ill too, and then, on the seventh day, I collapsed. I just needed more sleep than I was getting and with all the daily chores and work to do to keep the camp operating, it was too much. Once I got sorted with a normal bed, though, I was fine straight away.

The whole series only lasts nineteen days but it was tough in there, it really was, make no mistake. One aspect of the experience you probably don't appreciate when you are watching it on telly is the flies – millions of them, all over the gaff! You are sweating and being bitten all the time. You'd look down at your arm and there'd be a dozen flies sucking into it, so you'd wipe, scrape or pick them off as best you could and while you were doing that, they'd be landing on your other arm. It used to drive us all insane. When Brian Harvey did his challenge – having a million insects dropped onto him in a glass box – they first coated him with this spray that attracted flies like nobody's business. The problem was that when he came back to the camp, it seemed impossible to wash the gunk all off and that just made the flies miles worse, they were everywhere. I actually thought the crew was deliberately releasing the things. One day when I was feeling particularly desperate about this, I shouted, 'I can't take any more of these flies!' Joe just looked at me and said, 'Shut it!'

It was hard eating so little too – I went from 15-and-a-half stone to 13 stone in those nineteen days. It was hard having to do all that work every day too, and it was hard sleeping so little, and so on. Some of the days felt like they were lasting *forever*. But you know what? Having said all that, within a few minutes I was having the time of my life. I absolutely loved it in there.

As the days went by, the pressures on us became more and more harsh to the point where they were releasing rats into the site to liven us up at the end! During that time I did things you would never, ever expect to do. I jumped into a pool with three crocodiles in it and swam around with a snake around one arm and a croc swimming beneath me; I even got bitten twice by snakes – but it was all great! I did anything they threw at me, even lying in that glass box with God-knows-what crawling all over me. The challenges were brilliant – when I was talking to Joe about his tasks, I just said to him, 'Close your eyes, take yourself out of it, it is only two or three minutes out of your whole, entire life. Look at these challenges like that and you will be able to do anything.'

Antonio Fargas – aka Huggy Bear – was a legend. I had done the *Starsky & Hutch* movie première party at Trap and met him that night. He was wicked; I really liked him. Every evening me and Huggy would sit up chatting all night. We said we would stay in touch after the show but it is hard, especially with him being in the USA. He's a great character, though: I loved Huggy.

Joe was great too and deserved to win. When I saw that clip of me and him in the toilet with his finger virtually up my arse trying to find the insect bites, I was mortified! I thought, *I'm never going to live this down!* Joe just kept himself to himself, stayed away from the dramas, worked very hard and was a fantastic bloke. He was very nice to me, and about me, which was very kind. A few weeks after the jungle, Joe was doing a live show and we were chatting and he said, 'I learned more from you in those few weeks than I have from anyone in my whole life.' That was a lovely thing to hear.

Janet Street-Porter, I loved her. Janet's been there, she's done it all, she knew the whole score with Paul Burrell. She was just so clever and yet so approachable; I have a lot of time for her. She is a woman who doesn't give a shit if people don't like her – she didn't go there to make people like her. She only went there because John Lydon had and she thought she could stir it up a little too, which she did brilliantly. I think she was also writing while she was there, so she was working too! She was tough as well, Janet – she was out there getting bitten by snakes and never worried by it at all.

Me and Brian Harvey got on really well. Since the jungle we've been out a few times together and he is a lovely man. He'd just lost his grandmother when we landed in Australia, though, and she'd been a very major part of his life, so in retrospect there was no way he could have enjoyed that jungle experience, given his awful personal circumstances. Brian is a genuine bloke, but he is one of those people who has had some really shit things just happen to him, things he couldn't control, just life dealing him a tough hand. Sometimes people think he seems to struggle with day-to-day bits and bobs but to be honest, considering what he's been through, I think he does bloody well. I was gutted for him when he had that bad car accident shortly after *I'm A Celebrity*. Grieving like he was, the jungle was not an ideal place to be. When you lose someone dear to you, the emotions are running very high, you are not yourself; the jungle experience was so surreal, so bizarre, it was a lot for him to deal with. I think he left at exactly the right time because he could have done himself some damage. That said, I have got all the time in the world for him.

Sheila Ferguson was a nice woman. She's got two beautiful daughters who were over there supporting her. 'You stay away from my daughters, you lunatic!' she told me on one occasion. 'Imagine you as my son-in-law!' She was crazy, full of energy, although a couple of times she came across quite bossy, which didn't go down too well with some people. To be honest, I didn't have a problem with it except on one occasion: I'd been collecting wood and working like a dog for three hours up and down this hill, I was shattered. I came back into camp for a brief rest and Sheila said, 'Don't sit down! Get back down to the river, we need someone to put some water in this pot.' I bit my tongue – later someone asked, 'Why didn't you say something?' but it wasn't worth the stress. That show is a pressure-cooker situation where feelings could boil over, and I knew that Sheila was actually a lovely lady.

After I'd clarified with Sophie and her boyfriend about the tabloid speculation before we went into the jungle, I got on quite well with her. A few people were vexed by the fact that they thought she wasn't pulling her weight, but I didn't want to get involved in any of that. She is an all-right bird and I sometimes see her around town to say hello.

Vic Reeves didn't like me. I didn't know what had gone on until I got out of the show, but Nancy was saying to him, 'Oh, Fran's been flirting with me, trying it on,' and all that. That was one of the first things she said when they brought Vic in. I was like, 'What are you thinking?

We were having a joke! You are a married bird.' She was messing just the same; it was just a giggle.

When Vic arrived, I went to shake his hand and he turned his back on me. In all fairness, he never even gave me a chance and I was happy to apologise if something had been misconstrued, but I didn't think there was any need to turn his back on me when my hand was stretched out to shake his.

Natalie Appleton shouldn't have gone there. All her mates told her not to go and they were right. Natalie is a lovely, lovely girl, she really is, but she was just in a situation she shouldn't have been in. Having said that, the TV edits can be misleading on some occasions. You know that bit where she touched a tree and squealed? Well, I know she got a lot of stick for that reaction but, in all fairness, there was a reason why she was so alarmed by what she had done. Before we went into the jungle, we were briefed about various plants and animals and what risks we were facing. The experts told us certain types of trees had built up defence mechanisms and if you touched their bark they would attack you by shooting out dozens of spikes. One or two of the lads in the crew touched these trees and had to sit there and have fifty or so thorns pulled out of their hands. So when Natalie touched the tree, that's why she reacted that way.

At first, we thought she kept getting picked for tasks because people loved her. It was going on for a few days and I still hadn't done anything and I was thinking *Nat is going to get picked again. What is going on?* The problem was, she was coming home with less and less food every day. But you know what? No one out there was bitchy about it, and if anyone had said a word to her I'd have said, 'Shut up, this is what we came out here for!' Everyone stuck by her, and I wouldn't have a bad word said about her.

There is no question of who was the single most entertaining man out there, though: Paul Burrell. I love him, man! I have to say I wasn't a big fan beforehand, although that was based on very little real knowledge of him. Even my friend Adee had said in his salon before we flew out, 'Fran, the first two people out of the jungle will be Joe and Paul.' However, I grew to like Paul more and more with every day that passed. He worked hard, chatted with everyone; he was a gentleman.

The footage of Paul eating those insects and fish eyes and animal testicles was simply classic TV. I have never known someone to be so entertaining in my whole life – just look at the value those producers got out of him. It must have been the stuff of dreams. The man is a legend.

The one thing about Paul Burrell that is simply incredible is this: here is a man who could actually bring a nation down to its knees, if he wanted to. Do you know why I love him? Because he's a genuinely normal bastard who got thrown into the abyss! They chewed him up and spat him out – and he came back with a smile. You can't bring a man like that down. We are talking about the history of this country – after all, the Queen personally became involved to stop the court case in which he was accused of secretly hoarding some of Princess Diana's personal effects. Despite all of that, and everything that has happened to that man, he is still smiling. And that is a true testament to his character.

Worse still, people have such preconceived ideas about him: some hate him, they detest him, but they don't even know the first thing about him. I've since become good friends with Paul, his wife and his family and I have seen this ignorance first-hand. After I finished the programme I was in a bar in Marbella and this guy and his wife started telling me they thought he was a wanker. I said, 'You are wrong about Paul,' but this bloke wouldn't leave it, he just went on and on about hating him and why. I started to get angry with him because I found such an attitude towards someone I had come to regard as a close friend very upsetting, so I told him, 'Listen, I know him and he is not like that at all. You do your own thing but just don't say it in front of me!'

Another time I witnessed this kind of attitude, I was actually with Paul. I was walking with him and his wife through central London and this man came up and was being really abusive to him, swearing, being aggressive and confrontational. I stepped in and said, 'Listen, don't be rude, don't talk to my friends in that way,' but he carried on. We walked on but he walked alongside us, still swearing at Paul. I took him to one side, told Paul to walk on and had another quiet word – 'Don't say anything else, OK?' But straight away he began swearing in Paul's direction again. I'd had enough; he was too threatening. Boom! He spent the next twenty minutes or so spark out on the floor.

You have to be able to judge people on how you find them yourself. From having a small degree of dislike for Paul – due to what I'd been told or had heard in the press – I went to taking his kids out in London, dining out with him and his wife. I love them both. Paul made me promise to read at least three or four chapters of his book, so I did! But I already knew enough about the man to make my mind up by then.

Funnily enough, the time I really got to know Paul was on the flight back from the jungle, when he, Adee and myself spent twenty-six hours together, no cameras, no one else, just chatting. That's when I realised what a star he is. I have actually grown to love the man and respect him. When I launched a telephone directory enquiries service with a big TV advert in August 2005, Paul cancelled a whole session of filming to come down. He spent all day with my family and friends and supported me on that big occasion. When it really comes down to biting the crust off the biscuit for your friends, you'll either be there or you won't and Paul is the type who will be there. Paul Burrell is a legend: fact.

It's funny really, because working the doors of nightclubs couldn't be further away from being in the Australian jungle with a dozen celebrities for weeks on end with cameras on you 24/7. Yet all those years on the doors equipped me perfectly to deal with all the personal politics and personality clashes that arose during the show. It was the ideal training and that's why I think I was able to stay out of the fighting and arguing relatively easily.

Once I was down to the final three, I knew I was going to be third. I'd already done more than I could ever think possible. So much for having three weeks jet-skiing with me mates! Plus, Paul and Joe had had some serious fears and I think they both deserved to win. Joe was a gentleman and Paul had really come out of himself – as I said during the actual interview, 'Paul has done himself and his family proud. Out of everyone Joe has kept himself quiet and worked hard...'

When you are about to walk out of that jungle camp, it's one of the most bizarre feelings. You have been *totally* cut off from everything for nineteen days and even though you know people have liked you because you came third, you don't know anything about what has happened in the outside world. The crew can't talk to you at any point so you really do have no idea about what's been going on while you've been away. You literally do not know what you are about to walk into. One thing that does make me laugh is that a lot of women said I looked deadly when I was being interviewed by Ant and Dec, but I look at myself and think I look well rough.

I hung around the camp until Joe and Paul came out and we spoke to each other briefly, then headed back to the hotel. Adee had come over with me and was waiting for me when I came out. Mad bastard that he is, he said, 'When you come out of the jungle I will have a pint of Guinness, a steak or maybe some sausage and mash potatoes waiting for you.' And he bloody cooked that on the morning of every eviction day just in case it was me going home. And there he was with a Shepherd's Pie waiting – bloody tasty it was too, I tell you! Then we hopped in the car, cracked open some champagne and got drunk on the way back to the hotel. Oh yes, Adee had been living in a six-star Versace hotel in my room for two-and-a-half-weeks while I was starving out in the jungle! Mind you, because we had eaten so little, it was hard to have a big meal for quite a few days immediately after we came out of the jungle.

Adee asked me, 'Do you know how big this has been?' When I confessed that I didn't, he told me, 'Mate, your life has changed.' When we got to the hotel, the first thing they did was hand me a big bag of fan mail, which was very strange – I almost thought it must be for someone else. All the celebrities who'd already come out were in normal clothes, their hair washed and styled, it was really odd seeing them again like that. Everyone was doing all these big newspaper interviews – James rang and said, 'You've been offered *Now* magazine for six grand.' 'Nah, James,' I told him, 'I've just spent nineteen days in the jungle, I'm going to the pub!' I can imagine a few people might be laughing, 'no newspaper deal for Fran Cosgrave' and all that – whatever, I didn't give a shit. Adee, myself and a few doormen went out that night, got mashed and had to drag ourselves to the airport for the flight home the very next day – they boot you out within twenty-four hours.

I came home on 13 December and was stunned by the reaction from the public, even though certain people had sold negative stories about me in the papers. I knew a few people liked what they saw because I had come third, but people were so nice to me, shouting compliments at me in the street, winding car windows down to say hello, it was a really lovely feeling. One time, I was walking along the street and spotted three builders with a striped haircut like the one I had in the jungle. When they saw me, they were shouting 'Fran! Hey! All right?' and we had a little chat.

When I came back from the jungle, press attention had increased massively. Unfortunately, at the time Kerry Katona was very down, dead low and had been in The Priory. Even after me and Tash broke up, Kerry and me had stayed great mates. She was keen to take a break and I mentioned that I was going to Marbella with my family, Adee and Calum. Then Calum couldn't make it so I invited Kerry – it seemed like the perfect way for her to get some rest and relaxation among friends. Next thing I know, it's in the papers about mc and Kerry getting together.

I was horrified because of Tash, obviously, but also because I was friends with Bryan McFadden. I phoned Paul and he spoke with Bryan, who was really cool about it; he knows how the papers work. In the end, Kerry wasn't able to come on holiday with us because we knew paps would take pictures and writers would make stories out of it. She was upset about not being able to go, though; it was a shame. Even when Adee and me got to the airport, there were a load of paps waiting for a picture of me and Kerry. Then we flew out and there were even more waiting for the scoop at Marbella airport. Crazy!

My time in the jungle allowed people to judge me from actually seeing me, rather than hearing words out of other people's mouths or from reading newspaper articles. It was an incredible experience. And when you think the entire episode came about because of a twist of fate, because I bumped into that head of programming in a corridor one day, it's so weird. Looking back at those nineteen days now, though, it feels like a lifetime away.

The jungle was a pivotal experience for me. When I came out of there, I had a renewed belief that everyone can have a shot. If it can happen to me, it can happen to anyone. I'd always had drive and ambition and enjoyed really successful periods, but as I've said, just before I flew to Australia I was in a rut. I'd been low on confidence and direction, then flew out to Oz and had been thrown into all these odd and demanding situations and thought to myself, *Can you deal with this?* And the answer was 'Yes!' The jungle is one of the most deadly things that's ever happened to me, absolutely fantastic, because just at that moment in my life, I found something that had burnt its way out of me and, immediately prior to the show, had gone altogether. For the first time, I had felt like I could be defeated. I'd never felt like that before. When I came out of that jungle three weeks later, I felt invincible again; that I would never be beaten... the jungle got that feeling back for me. I would give anything to be able to relive that time of my life.

# CHAPTER SEVENTEEN

# PARADISE AROUND THE CORNER

When I came back from the jungle, you'd have thought I'd have taken the opportunity to step back from all the madness that had made me so depressed just before I'd flown out to Australia – not so. I returned to London and plunged right back into the insanity of clubland. I was out every night again, partying, my head still full of business issues, things to do, people to see, it was just mad again, almost within minutes of touching down at Heathrow. Obviously, having been on the TV meant there were even more things to do, with appearances, interviews and such like, but at times it was almost like *I'm A Celebrity...* had never happened.

One night I was out in Hoxton with friends in a bar. We'd been out all night long and then headed straight to a pub to continue. I was having a chat when I looked up and there in front of me was the female manager of Home, who had given me that door job years ago. I wouldn't say we left on bad terms, although we obviously disagreed, but to be fair it was quite nice to see her – she was managing that bar in Hoxton now. What was really funny was that while we were there, this guy kicked off at the door and I had to go and sort it out! I couldn't help myself and we did exchange a wry smile. It was like nothing had changed.

However, after the jungle it was clear that working on doors was probably not going to be a job I could do any longer. Then the phone rang and it was James again: 'Fran, how would you feel about flying out to a desert island for five weeks?' The people who ran *I'm A Celebrity...* had called James up – they were doing a new programme out in Fiji and would I be interested? I must be one of the luckiest people alive. How many other people get off one huge reality TV show and within three months are invited onto another massive show? Well, that's what happened to me within twelve weeks of returning from the jungle; those girls at ITV have really put their wings over me, and I thank them heartily for that. I don't know why they did it, but all I can say is that they must have taken a shine to me.

At first, I assumed there was some element of survival out there, like we'd have to build our own huts or rafts and catch our own food, fend for ourselves, that sort of thing. I really fancied that. Then James said, 'No, Fran, they want you to go and live on a desert island in the lap of luxury with five single women for weeks, just chilling, and try and fall in love with someone.' I couldn't quite believe my ears! And the best part was, they were going to pay me to do it. Unlike *I'm A Celebrity...* right from the start there was no way I was going to say no to this. When they said we'd get picked to go on 'dates' with each other, I did wonder if it was my cup of tea after all, but the thought of all that time away from the madness was just too tempting: 'Sign me up for Fiji!'

Although I personally had no qualms about going to a desert island for a few weeks of pure indulgence, the programme makers were taking something of a gamble. It was a format that hadn't been tried before and no one knew if it was going to work or not or even knew if anything would happen that was interesting enough to make a programme out of. One night I got chatting to Calum Best about it and said, 'Mate, you have got to get yourself on this programme.' In fact, ITV had already thought about approaching him, so when he told me he was going too, I was delighted. For ages I was trying to persuade them to take Adee too, then we'd have been three lunatics out there, having a blast, but they said it wouldn't have worked because there'd be too many people who knew each other already. I think they were just scared of us wrecking the gaff! That was a great shame, because Adee is a very entertaining guy.

Myself and Calum Best are very similar but also very different. Over the years, we have had some wild, wild times. Mentallers! We had to stop hanging out for a while because we were egging each other on, with women, clubbing, partying, regularly taking two days on the piss. At one point we ended up drinking gin out of a teapot, during a great night out that continued until the end of the week. Rampaging, deadly nights. Me, Calum and Adee are like the Three Musketeers. We have a really good lads' buzz when we go on the piss.

Perhaps surprisingly, the three of us rarely dig into the dark things in our lives and personal problems when we're together; our friendship has been built on simply going out and enjoying ourselves. I know when I am out with either or both of them that we won't be sitting there wrecking each other's heads with all the shit we've been going through. That is an escape in itself.

Both Calum and Adee are regular travellers on what I like to call my choo-choo train of life. I have been in London for quite a few years now and I always feel like I'm driving some insane bullet-train going round and round town, partying, never stopping. Over the years, dozens of people have hopped on board, some for a short trip, others a long ride, but always I am at the front, leading the journey. A lot of people have fallen by the wayside, and a lot of people are still clinging on for dear life!

We know we won't be partying every night forever. Me and Calum have got this dream with a few of the lads: if we can make fifty or sixty years old in one piece and be sitting on a beach with a cold bottle of beer, our kids around us, watching the sun go down, we'll be happy men. For years I have had this image inside of me that that's where I'm going to end up.

Fortunately for me, I was about to experience a small

taste of this dream shortly when I flew out to Fiji. I didn't know who else was going, they kept it all very secretive, but then I heard that Liz McClarnon from Atomic Kitten was going and I was like, 'No way!' Given that the show was essentially a spin on the dating game and that the love of my life, Tash, who I still missed terribly, was Liz's band mate, this was all very awkward. Plus part of the appeal of Fiji was the chance to get away from it all, to clear my head and re-evaluate my life – yet I was actually going to be spending weeks with my ex's best mate. I love Liz, don't get me wrong, she is a deadly girl, but it just unsettled me a little when I first heard. Let's just say, me and Liz as an item was never going to happen, as I am sure she will agree; we are just such good mates.

The day before we were leaving, me and Calum went for a few gargles and had a deadly night out, a really good time. That evening we got chatting to some girls and didn't actually go to bed at all. We grabbed some breakfast, drove over to Adee's so he could do my hair for the trip and then I dashed across town to my flat in the Docklands and threw a load of clothes in a suitcase – making sure I had the key to the lock this time. Then I jumped in a taxi to drive straight to the airport. I arrived at check-in to meet the ITV girls in a jock, but I was so excited I felt brilliant.

The plane was delayed for about forty minutes and as we all sat there waiting for the signal to take off, I got chatting to this guy sitting next to me. He was in his sixties, I think, and a really interesting bloke. We talked about all sorts of things and, when the plane finally took off, we carried on chatting non-stop for twelve hours. He told me about his family and his business, I was telling him what I was up to, my granddad, life stories and such like, and I really enjoyed the conversation. Those long-haul flights can be a real bore, but talking to this guy for the first leg made the time rush past.

The amazing thing was, about three weeks into *Celebrity Love Island*, they gave us all letters from loved ones and friends. I opened one of these to find it was from this very same chap I'd been talking to on the plane over. He'd tracked me down to the island in Fiji and managed to get an email through to the ITV people. In the letter he said he'd really enjoyed meeting me, that all his daughters were fans and that if the programme showed the public a fraction of the personality he had seen on that flight, then I was sure to win. I was so flattered and touched that he had gone to so much trouble to get in touch and then to say such nice things, I thought that was amazing. The funny thing was, on the second leg of the flight, when this older man had changed to get his connection, his seat was taken up by a much younger guy. I just knew we had nothing in common, so we both put our headsets on and didn't say a word to each other (just as, when I flew to the jungle, I had listened to Kittens songs all the way, thinking of Tash and Josh). Isn't it strange how you have such instant chemistry with certain people, though? I love it when that happens.

Every long-haul journey I take, I seem to either meet someone who makes me think about life or I just sit there mulling it all over for myself. You have such a long time to think about things and, for once, my phone doesn't ring, I don't need to be somewhere else, I can just sit there and muse over stuff. I actually really enjoy long haul, although that's probably to do with the fact that at least two of those big flights have sent me off to foreign climes and into situations that have totally changed my life for the better. As soon as I buckle up, I get this feeling of anticipation and excitement about the adventure ahead; I can't tell you how much I love that feeling.

When I was making my connection, I went to the shops but for some reason my credit card wasn't working. So now I had no money and it was hours before my connecting flight. I asked if there was a gym I could use but there wasn't, so I was bored off my tits. Eventually, I got chatting to this security guard who told me they had a treadmill in the staff quarters and he let me go in there and use it! I passed the time away running miles on this staff treadmill for three hours – it was all rather weird.

Arriving somewhere I've never been before is one of the things I love most in life. That moment when you step off the plane or boat onto new ground is so exciting – magical. Within seconds of setting foot in Fiji, I knew it was going to be one of the most beautiful places I had ever seen. When I got to my transfer, the whole crew were the same as the ones in the jungle, and they were all shouting out to me, 'Hey Fran! How did you manage this one as well?' They were a great crowd.

I got in this car, took my shirt off and started catching some sun and thought to myself, *Oh my God, this is the life!* We drove for about half an hour through the most amazing countryside down to the docks where a boat was waiting to take me to the island. It was a really big vessel, with a canopy at the back – and the bloody thing could shift! I stood at the back for the fifty-minute journey, hanging onto the canopy, with the sun on my skin, the blue water all around me and I just couldn't believe my luck. We rushed off into the sea and already I was thinking *This is the nicest place I have ever seen.* Mind you, at one point, I was dangling my feet into the cool blue water and a boat-hand said, 'I wouldn't do that if I were you, there's a few things down there that might fancy a nibble... dangerous stuff, sir.'

It was two days before the programme was due to start, so they first took us to a stop-off island, not that this was any less luxurious. It was called Bounty Island and it was incredible; it just kept getting better. They were meant to keep us apart before the show started but there was no way they could separate me and Besty so we had a couple of deadly nights. When I first clapped eyes on Calum, I must have looked a sight because I'd been training hard and was well pumped up. When he saw me he was like, 'Jesus! Look at you! This place is amazing, isn't it?' We went for a walk barefoot on the beach and just kept looking and sniggering at each other. It was brilliant, two best mates out there, getting paid to be in this heaven on earth.

All the security guards knew of me in advance again, but after we'd drunk them under the table on the local spirit – guava, which I believe is illegal in the UK because of its hallucinogenic properties – we were all the best of friends. The woman who ran the resort was this lovely Scottish bird and she took me in a golf cart to my luxury bedroom hut, which overlooked these mountains and a lake with the clearest water you've ever seen. The windows were just mesh because the weather was always so good, the furniture was gorgeous, the kitchen was amazing, there were two bottles of champagne on ice... I was almost in a daze by this point.

The night before we were due to go into the island, I had a nice quiet meal and went to bed early, but I couldn't sleep. I was tossing and turning, but it was no use, so I went for a run around the island in the moonlight. Every now and then a flying fish would leap out of the black water and then splash back down; it was magical. I stood at the end of this wooden jetty, drinking in the fresh air, listening to the sounds and the silence. It was beautiful, and it made me think, *I wish Tash and Josh were here with me...*

# CHAPTER EIGHTEEN

# TOES IN THE WATER, THOUGHTS BACK HOME

They told us the plan was for all the men to jet-ski into the island. Although I'd done this loads of times before, not everyone on the show had, so we were all given lessons. To their credit, they didn't just give us crappy old jet-skis and let us loose in a pool; they gave us these brilliant jet-skis and sent us out into the middle of the bloody ocean for five hours! That's when I first started to think that Paul Danan was a lunatic – and I don't necessarily mean in a funny way! I'd seen him around town in London a few times but never really spoken with him at length. I could just tell he was going to be a mentaller.

Obviously there were rules to follow for the safe use of the jet-skis, rules you had to abide by. Every time I went to talk to Besty, Paul revved his engine loudly and soaked us, which was funny for about two seconds. What a dootz! We went out and there was a press boat in the sea capturing photos of us all. So in turn, we each skied up close to them, waving and all that shit; but when it came to Paul Danan's turn, he went flying towards them. We were all shouting, 'Paul, slow down!' and as he got close by he swerved and absolutely soaked all of the press pack. They were going nuts, waving their fists and shouting at him and I was just thinking *He's not all there, he's not fully switched on.* I could tell it was going to blow up with him when we got in there.

Right before we went in, we met the staff and loads of them thought we were film stars shooting on location. I didn't have the heart to tell them otherwise and neither did Calum, so when they said to him, 'Which part are you playing?' he coolly replied, 'I'm playing myself.' I didn't venture to ask if they thought I was Jean-Claude Van Damme.

Then, finally, we jet-skied into the island one by one, Besty first. Bearing in mind it was some form of dating show, I'd like to report that I was up for some romance, but as soon as I met all the ladies I realised I wasn't going to fancy any of them. Some of the contestants were saying they'd only be there for a week, but I wasn't interested in that – I wanted to stay for the full term.

We picked our beds and Besty and myself got one beside each other, which was a right laugh. We all thought there would be loads of alcohol and partying all night long, right from the off. Me and Besty were planning on drinking piña coladas for the first morning's sunrise but we walked in, went straight to the bar and it was empty – no food or drink. They wouldn't give us any drink for the first four days, apparently. We were going mad, and I was convinced we'd all been stitched up, that this 'luxury' island trip was all a big scam and that actually they were going to let us fend for ourselves after all. I got hold of one of the ITV crew and asked, 'Where are all these free drinks that you promised us?' 'It's the first day, no drinks I'm afraid, Fran,' she replied. I reported back to Calum and said, 'We've been dumped on Detox Island, Besty.' Instead of piña coladas and partying, that first night we ended up playing charades stone cold sober. The second night they gave us one beer – now I use one beer to brush my teeth. At that point, I thought the whole experience was going to go on forever. I worked out a lot to fill the days because if you weren't sent on a day trip, it could be quite boring finding something to do. When I travelled out there I was already in great shape but by the time I'd eaten, slept and trained well for five weeks I was possibly in the best shape of my life. I went running every day too and by the end I felt like a million dollars.

It was a good bunch of people on the island. I'd met Lee Sharpe briefly before, and obviously with what he'd done at Man United he is a legend. I got on quite well with him but clearly there was a lot going on with Jayne Middlemiss and Abi Titmuss. He's a great bloke, though: I liked Lee.

Du'aine Ladejo was sound, I really got on with him straight away. He was into his training and I liked all that. I think he had some strange days out when he went off on trips but for me he was a nice guy and I was sad to see him leave. I've been out with him a good few times since we got back.

Michael Greco's dad had died shortly before he went out to Fiji and, just like Brain Harvey beforehand, it made life very testing for him. At least Fiji was a much easier ride than the jungle, but at the same time when you are grieving for such a close family member, your world is turned upside down and maybe being on a reality TV show isn't the easiest task to face in such circumstances. He had a really hard time with that, understandably. At the start he seemed to like Abi and there was a bit of interest there for the viewers I think, but again I kept myself out of the way. I was too busy relaxing!

Paul Danan is a nice kid but he went a bit mad when he had a few jars in him. A few times, me and him would go head to head after he got a bit drunk. Good job he didn't go to Night Owls as a punter! We were sitting by the pool one day and Paul was talking to Nicki, the American girl who came in after everyone else, and he said, casual as you like, 'So how's Justin and Cameron getting on?' I pissed myself laughing, it was ridiculous. Mate, shut up!

Two of the women were always going to be a no-no. Obviously Liz is a close friend of mine and Tash's, but Isabella Hervey was also one of Jodie Marsh's best friends. I'd only bumped into her once in London and she completely blanked me. There was quite a bit of tension between us at first but eventually we got on fairly well. I thought she was attractive, she had a great body and I liked the fact that she trained so hard.

I'd never met Jayne before but I very quickly grew to like her a lot and we got on well. I have to say I thought of her mostly more as a mate or a sister than a potential girlfriend. Having said that, there were a couple of occasions in the Love Shack when I caught myself thinking, *I actually might like Jayne in another way...* but nothing ever developed from that. Besides, my thoughts were always with Tash back in the UK. No one was ever going to compare to Tash. Jayne 'Middlesex', as I call her, is a lovely bird and I've been out with her a few times since we got back.

Abi is a weird one. To be honest, she is a nice girl and she's done well for herself, but I am not really into all that press lark; I stay away from it as much as I can. Abi seemed really into all that malarkey, but that whole glamour thing in the papers is of no interest to me. I don't want to live my life through newspapers. To be honest with you, I thought her relationship with Lee was for the cameras, but that's just my opinion. We were all watching that and were pretty suspicious really, but I think our concerns came across. Conversations would be started and you could tell what people thought.

It was strange watching Isabella and Paul too. I think the whole thing with Paul was disgraceful, you shouldn't take that off anyone, never mind someone you don't really know... and especially not on a TV show when everyone is watching you. I was embarrassed, but it was none of my business to get involved. You are stuck on an island in a confined space and the guy is trying it on with every single bird! Then Nicki Ziering arrived and disappeared into the toilets and slept for three days. It was like she was never really there – so then Paul got it on with her. It was nuts. I wish she could have smelt the coffee. Paul tried it on with Rebecca, Abi, everyone! Abi said they didn't do anything but we were watching when they were in the pool and they were snogging, let me tell you. I don't care what she says. She'll kill me for saying that, but they were.

Judi Shekoni was kicked out the first week, but then no one went for some time. After a while, we were writing everyone's name on the wall and we'd forgotten about her because she went so early. I knew Judi from partying in London and she is a nice girl, but I think when she started talking about LA, with a slight American note to her accent, some people took against her. That was unfortunate, but Irish and English people don't really care for all that. I guessed she would be the first person out for that reason.

I could tell with Liz that the producers really wanted us two to get together, but it wasn't going to happen. When we were in the Love Shack it was cool because we are just good pals and had a nice time, chilled out with some cocktails and had some nice dinner. Paul was stirring it, saying, 'I think you and Liz are a perfect couple,' and I was like, 'Don't fuck around with family, that's not on!' Imagine if Liz and I had got together, it would have caused so much trouble. It would have been *Murder She Wrote*, and who could solve the mystery of the disappearing Irishman.

I'd never met Rebecca Loos before either. Before I went there I wasn't sure what to make of her. I hate the whole stories-in-the-tabloids world; it really winds me up. She spoke about Beckham a few times but I just switched off to it. She is an all right bird, actually, I got on quite well with her; she has got something about her that draws you to her, I can't explain what it is. Objectively, she is quite attractive, although I wasn't attracted to her personally, if you understand what I am saying. I think the fact she was messing around with Calum had something to do with him going so early; I'm not sure people were comfortable with that. The night he got kicked off, she got smashed with Abi and was sitting on the bed by me saying, 'Don't be scared of me,' and I said, 'I'm not, believe me!' She was steaming drunk – though, to be fair, it was harmless. Quite a few of the girls told me they thought I was all sensitive and a deep thinker when I was away from the lads, but I totally refuted that!

Ironically, as I have mentioned, my level of tolerance towards people taking the piss has come down a lot recently. I don't know if I could work the door any more. I expect people to have more respect, especially in a situation like the one in Fiji. When Paul Danan was in my face that night when we argued, it was hard to be calm and restrained. It was all because of Abi – she'd said, 'Leave him alone' but I was standing up for her, so I said, 'Shut up!' I couldn't believe I'd said that myself, actually, but the context was so ridiculous, it was such a surreal environment. But Danan kept going at me, right in my face. In my life now I try to hold back any feelings of aggression, but in years gone by, I would have politely escorted him to the floor. There is a very, very good chance he would have *slipped*. He was car-crash TV, he really was. I think he could have won if he had kept being entertaining instead of getting aggressive and abusive.

I wasn't sure who would win at first, although if Paul and Isabella had stayed together they would have. I could barely believe it when I got to the last day. I love Liz and Jayne both, so either one would have been great as a winner. When they said Jayne was the female winner, I obviously assumed it would be with Lee, so I put my head down and readied myself to congratulate him. When they said my name, I was stunned; I couldn't talk. During the interview immediately afterwards, I kept saying to myself, 'Talk! Talk!' but then I was worried I would say something stupid. I was shaking; it was so shocking. Immediately after, I sat on the beach with Calum and he said, 'Mate, you've won!' It wasn't until a few weeks later at a service station in the UK that it actually sunk in: I had won. Amazing!

When they did the wrap party, I celebrated hard. It had been weeks since I'd had a proper drink but instead of just having a nice, relaxing drink or two, I got mashed. I got stuck into a bottle of Jack Daniel's with Calum and that was the end of the story. I went up onto a second-floor balcony and jumped off it into the pool, not realising I was heading for the shallow end, so I smashed my ankle up really badly and could barely walk. All the security guys picked me up out of the pool, but fortunately I didn't feel any pain until the next day.

I pissed myself off a little bit because I wished I'd stayed a bit more sober for that party. People were making little speeches and having a great time – I got up to say a few words and you could almost hear people collectively take a breath and say, 'What is the lunatic Irishman going to say?' I don't remember my exact words, but I do recall getting a very nice ovation, which was the perfect way to round the experience off.

I've done well most of my life but I've never really won anything like that (apart from the prize for my 'Santa Claws' story as an eight-year-old, that is). Third in the jungle was good enough for me, but to win *Love Island* was unbelievable. A nice reality let me tell you. The sense of wellbeing was amazing, but I suppose weeks and weeks on a luxury desert island is going to do that to you. I could cope with a reality like that every day!

After the jungle and Fiji I started doing what are known as 'PAs'. Usually this entailed me going to a club and, more often than not, DJ-ing; sometimes, though, they just want me to say hello to people. It's not something I ever thought I would do, to be honest. They are mental occasions, though, absolutely mental. Sometimes it's a bit scary – like in September 2005 in Glasgow when things got way out of hand. For someone like me who was paid to keep things under control for so many years, it is easy to spot when a situation is spiralling into chaos. And when it does, believe me, it is quite frightening.

I knew I was going to get a good reception because during the day I had been in town and met loads of people. At one point, a big gang of about forty lads, all in football shirts, came up to me and I wasn't sure what was going to happen. Fortunately, they just wanted to say hello and shake my hand. It was great. One of them said to me, 'Do you know what I like about you? You are not trying to be a TV presenter or anything like one of them wankers off *Big Brother*, you are still being yourself after the show.' It's true, I didn't go on the show to try and become something else. I went on the show to be myself, then I came off and I am still myself.

I went to this club for a PA on the night and the doormen were lovely. They were talking me up, saying they'd had all sorts of celebrities there but nothing like the pandemonium that night. It was very strange for me because it was exactly like what I'd seen when I was working for Westlife. Unfortunately, at one point there was a massive crush downstairs and people were falling over and getting trodden on, girls were crying and it was very scary indeed. I was in the middle of all this and the doormen were trying to drag me off, even though my instinct was to start barking orders and try to resolve the panic. But I realise that however much it goes against the grain, I have to pull away from that now, it would just cause absolute mayhem. It's a very unnatural thing for me to have to do, believe me.

Eventually, the situation was quelled and thankfully no one seriously hurt. Afterwards, when I told people about it, some of them said how nice it must be to have folks going so crazy to meet me. To be honest, events like that are just frightening, but in general I don't really pay any attention to it. By that, I don't mean the people – I will always stand and chat and have a laugh with people, especially if they have been so kind as to come and see me at a club or something. What I mean is I don't pay any attention to whether these 'fans' – for want of a better word – make me a better person than the next man. It is not real; I cannot bring all these people screaming and shouting at me into my normal life.

I often wonder how ordinary people from the street who do reality shows and become famous overnight can cope. Until the point at which they are thrust out into the public gaze, they will have had almost no experience of celebrity or fame. Though I don't see myself as a celebrity, I have been around celebrity for years. I watched the way people reacted around Westlife, how the machine worked, how they behaved, what the fans expected or were surprised by. It is a complex world to enter and to do so overnight is not something I'd want to tackle. I really do not think these people understand the Pandora's box they might be opening when they apply to these shows.

Fortunately, before I did any TV, I'd had years to build up an awareness of what kind of life this might lead to.

I'd seen it with Westlife, with Tash, with all the celebrities who came to my clubs, and so on. It was a known quantity to me. I believe I know how to cope with it – time will tell, of course, but I believe I do.

It all comes down to dignity. You can quite easily see the people who just want to be famous for the sake of it, shagging around, getting their tits out. People can see through that. Being in the public eye is not something that can be part of the fabric of your day-to-day life or a building block of your personality. Me and Tash don't sit there chatting about being a celebrity or not. For us the reality is if my alarm goes off at 6am instead of hers for a change, because I've got a TV show to do. If you take one impression of me away from this book, let it be that I do not put up a front. I do not 'act' in my public life. Hopefully, that's why the public have been so kind to me – they know there's no pretence, no charade.

People's reactions to me actually remind me of my roots and stop me getting carried away with the fame game. Almost without exception people are nice to me. There are a few times when things are said, but it's rare. I was in a VIP club in Dublin called Lilly's Bordello – this was before I'd even been on TV – and I heard one of the lads taking the piss and saying, 'Who the fuck does he think he is?' I turned round to him and said, 'I think I am the same as I always was. You've changed, not me.'

To be honest, I don't really get that kind of treatment very much. Hardly ever, really. 'Hometown boy done good' is how most Irish seem to see it. I am not some jumped-up prick, and I don't pay too much attention to celebrity. In fact, I don't think most people consider me a celebrity; that's the thing. Most of them just see me as a normal bloke who's done well for himself.

For most people fame will only exist as long as you are popular and you need to have something else going on ready for that moment when people might stop coming to see you. Without that and a perspective on fame and celebrity, once you are out of the spotlight, you'll be cast adrift.

After I came out of *Love Island*, I didn't do any interviews, just as when I left the jungle. They just want you to slag off the people you were with and say horrible things. But I'm just not going to do it. I was offered a substantial amount of cash, but I thought for a second and then said, 'Sorry, I've just won fifty grand, no need.'

When I first went back to Ireland after Fiji, the reaction was insane, far more mental than after the jungle. Girls were running out of shops to shout after me and everyone was so complimentary. I seemed to make them smile. Typically, the first evening on the town was no ordinary night out. I'd been out to see Kerry from the Kittens, who was taking a rest at this retreat, and the same evening I went out with Barry and had a great time. We went back to his house afterwards for a drink and eventually everyone fell asleep. I was spark out on the couch and the next morning, this bird said to me: 'A bloke just tried to open your trousers...' I went nuts! I was looking for this bloke and went into Barry's bedroom but no one had seen him. It turned out this guy went up to the top floor and got in bed with Barry's flatmate.

I rolled Barry out of the bed and said, 'We are going to see U2, come on!' We'd got hold of some tickets for the last concert of their current tour and it was the very first time I had been out in public in Dublin since Fiji. I wasn't entirely sure how people would react, but they couldn't have been nicer. Dublin people have been very good to me.

Then, in August 2005, I was invited to co-present a huge festival in Dublin's Phoenix Park, where loads of cool bands were playing. I must admit it was amazing to be standing on stage chatting to one hundred and twenty thousand people. That audience gave me the biggest cheers I'd ever had in my life. I was particularly struck by the fact that all the security men working that day were so nice to me, shouting after me, even asking for my autograph. I could see they were pleased that someone from their ranks had made it across 'to the other side', so to speak. I don't want to patronise anybody, but one of them said it made them think it could happen to any of them. It was such a homecoming and made me realise how lucky I am that the Irish support me like they do.

For me, the greatest reward from Fiji is not the prize money or the work it has created for me, it's the way people treat me now. The greatest value is making people smile, making them happy. It might sound like a cliché, but that's something I've been striving for since those days back at school in Dublin.

# CHAPTER NINETEEN

# WHOLE AGAIN

For a long time in my life, I was in a blur of work, partying, pressing on, total madness; when I came back from the jungle I plunged straight back into it. But when I returned from Fiji, I knew I had a chance to change my life, to take a step back and see where I had reached. *Love Island* was just one of the most eye-opening experiences I've ever had in my life. I had so much time to think about all that was happening in my world and what I wanted to do and how to do it. I'd finally been given the chance to clear my mind. In turn, Fiji gave me the opportunity to change my life. That show could change everything for my family, my kids and my closest friends.

I had never stopped thinking about Tash ever since we broke up. That will probably upset a few people but I have to be honest, I just couldn't stop. I always said to my mates when we broke up, 'I don't know how but I am going to get back with Tash some day.' Just before Fiji, I had closed myself off to wanting to be happy and have a relationship. When I was out there, though, I just couldn't stop thinking about her the whole time. There were so many moments of peace and relaxation on that island – it was the first time in as long as I can remember that I actually had calm: the train had finally stopped.

When I was there I was asked what I had discovered anything about myself and I replied, 'I know this sounds mad and I am going to get slagged off by all me mates, but it's made me realise I want someone back in my life.' With Liz being out there too, it brought it home to me, and made me think about Tash even more. Every single thing I do I take something away from it, an experience, a lesson... The lesson from Fiji was that I couldn't be without Tash in my life. One of the first messages I got after I'd won the show was a congratulations note from Tash and I can't tell you how pleased I was to get it.

I came back from Fiji wanting Tash in my life again more than ever. If I hadn't had those five weeks of peace and calm, I don't know where my head would have been. I wanted Tash; it was a single-minded, black-and-white issue. I told Mom and Dad, 'I have to have Tash back.' No matter what else was going to happen in my life, I couldn't have continued without having at least one more attempt at getting her back, to make it work. If she wasn't interested, at least I would know for sure – and then perhaps I would be able to find a way to carry on with my life.

I spoke to Tash on the phone. She had just separated from Gavin, so I was anxious not to take the piss out of anyone. Obviously I had to see her when I visited Josh or when he came to stay with me, and I was just relishing being around her again. Then, one day, I just came out with it – I told her how I felt. There was no point denying it any longer. That was a big thing. I can't tell you how happy I was when she said she wanted to get back together with me too!

It's strange because it felt like we never broke up. Tash has lived with another man and had a baby with him, yet I was still completely just head over heels in love with her and it felt perfect, like nothing was different. Except this time I was going to do everything in my power to keep us together permanently.

After being on those two reality TV shows, I do occasionally get invited to award ceremonies and other television functions. I'm not a big fan of these things, to be honest, but Tash and me often had a good night out and it is always good to see old friends. In September 2005, we were invited to the TV Quick Awards at The Dorchester hotel. We got really dressed up for the evening, I was in a £2,000 suit, Tash's Jimmy Choo shoes alone cost £800. She was in a beautiful dress and looked like a film star. We were both looking forward to a good night.

The ceremony itself went well, but then afterwards we were chatting with some friends when this bloke walked over to me unannounced, tapped me on the shoulder by way of introduction, interrupted our conversation and said, 'If there was an award for the worst haircut, you'd win it!' Although I was offended by his rudeness, I simply turned round and said, 'Thanks very much, sir,' and carried on speaking with my friends in what had been a private conversation.

Then another tap on the shoulder:

'You're not even a celebrity...'

'Thank you very much, again,' I said and turned back once more.

He was still there, wittering on, so I said to Tash, 'Let's go for a walk.' We started to move away, but as we did, I looked at Tash and said, 'Nah! I'm going to go back to him' and – although she will always look to avoid a confrontation – on this occasion she said, 'Fran, he was a total wanker. Let's do it.'

I walked up to this bloke's group of about six friends and straight away one of his mates started giving me all the 'Leave it!' routine. As he did so, I went as if to put my hand on his shoulder but 'accidentally' caught his face with my arm, after which he seemed to quieten down a bit. I turned to the guy, who had been mocking me a few minutes previously, and asked him, 'Excuse me, but what do you do?'

'Nothing,' he said.

'No, come on, what do you do?'

'Nothing.'

'Look,' I said, 'in all fairness, you've just pure abused me. What do you do?'

He couldn't believe I had gone back to speak to him – those people don't. Ignoring me, he shouted, 'Security! Security!'

'You clown! Security – what? You think they are going to sort me out? No, they're not, mate!'

Two security guards made as if to come over and as they did, I said, 'Hello lads, what's the story? Don't worry about this, I'm only having a chat.' They said, 'Hey Fran! How's it going? Cool.' And they stood where they were, coming no closer.

This bloke's face drained pasty white right in front of our eyes. I swear I saw his bottom lip start to wobble.

Turning back to him, I said, 'If you only had respect for yourself you wouldn't say things like that to a complete stranger like me. You are rude. I don't know who you are or what you do, and it doesn't matter what you perceive me to be, you are just rude. I don't like rude people.' This went on for a bit and when I had said my piece I took his dickie bow and pulled it back as far as my shoulder, I'm not joking. He was looking at my fingers clasping this dickie bow with great anxiety, waiting to see whether I would let it go... then SNAP! 'See you later.' He'd pure shit himself.

The thing is, I will always try and avoid face-offs like that. The problem was he'd gone out of his way to be abusive, thinking there would be no consequence to his actions. What he did was pure bullying, and I don't take that any more. Perhaps I'm less tolerant around rudeness now because I don't work the doors any more and so I'm less immune to it; maybe it's just not as acceptable to me any more. But mate, choose your enemy wisely. Of all the people to pick on that night, he chose a psychopathic Irishman – out of a room full of TV executives! Please! Not a good idea!

Anyway, me and Tash went into another room and some of his mates came over and said, 'We're so sorry, he's a prick.' When I walked out at the end of the night, I looked at him and he started to take his dickie bow off! Prick!

By contrast, outside the award ceremony there were loads of paps, naturally, and they were so nice to me – they really were. A lot of people hate them and think they are scumbags, but that's so unfair. People forget I used to be a doorman and as such I would stand outside the clubs for hour after hour talking to those guys while they waited for their money shot.

Then when me and Tash first started going out together but before it was common knowledge we would get out of cars and the paps were all there ready. But I would say, 'Please lads, don't take a picture because we'll get in loads of trouble,' and they'd all put their cameras down and let us walk through.

Before I did any TV myself, I would go to a première with Tash and I'd just stand to one side while they got their pictures of her and other celebs. I'd stand there for ages on quiet nights, chatting, asking them about their families, their jobs, how they were doing. Once I'd been on telly and they had to get snaps of me for some magazines – especially once I was back with Tash – they remained very respectful. They do their job and at the end of the day they know I'm not as interesting as other people are to them. If Josh is with us they usually ask if it is OK; we still enjoy a very friendly relationship with them. When Josh was born, some of the paps even bought him presents! They are only doing their job, after all, and it can be a very hard job at times. They've always been good to me, so I have a lot of time for them.

We got back together and had some wicked times again, but unfortunately it just didn't work when we were together as a couple, so we decided to split up in the middle of February 2006.

I was heart-broken, I'm not going to pretend otherwise. It was hell going through the split again and I was obviously extremely worried about making sure Josh wasn't unsettled. What I will say is that at least we tried, we went with our hearts and had some fantastic times together. I wouldn't change it for the world and I feel lucky that I got to spend that extra time with Tash. Plus I've got Josh and Harry who are just fantastic – although Harry is not my kid I have spent the last year with him and I have a great relationship both with him and Josh. I am very proud and lucky to be involved with those two beautiful kids and I love looking after them.

# EPILOGUE

Sometimes I feel a little tarnished by clubs now, to be honest with you. They have the capacity to suck up people's souls and occasionally, that can destroy folks. It's madness twenty-four hours a day; clubland can be the best – and worst – time of your life. Having said that, and as much as I am looking forward to new horizons, nightclubs will always be in my blood, as sure as the air that I breathe.

What did I want to do when I grew up? Be a DJ. Simple as that, make people dance. Well, those childhood dreams were left behind when the door work led to behind-the-scenes involvement in clubs and, much later, television. The irony is, of course, that after diverting my attentions away from DJ-ing, after all the TV shows, clubs and madness, I now regularly DJ in clubs all over the country. Sometimes there will be several thousand people watching my set, going nuts and I get paid more for one night than I used to receive for two or three months' scrapping at Night Owls. The first time Tash saw me DJ since we got back together in 2005, the place was rocking! She said to me, 'I don't know how you do it, but everything you always say you are going to do, you eventually do it.' That was a nice thing for her to say, and for me to hear. It's quite absurd really, the way it has all come full circle with the DJ-ing, and I will never, ever take that for granted. Weirder still, in the autumn of 2005, I signed a record deal, a dream I have had since I was a small kid. I have started to get my own studio built and after all these years, I can finally get down to releasing some cool tunes of my own.

I'm a lucky bastard. And I'm privileged people out there seem to like me. One thing I do in life is treat people nicely. Something that keeps me going when times are hard is when people come up to me in the street with a smile on their face because then I know that any mud-slinging just hasn't worked.

So many moments have been pivotal. Starting training, getting a job, quitting the gym to go on holiday, getting my badge in Westminster not Croydon, leaving Home, jumping out of that airplane, sitting on that jetty in Fiji and thinking of Tash, they are all decisions that changed my life. When I left Ireland to move to London, however, that was when I truly started to grow in confidence, when everything really began to change. So many people were expecting me to fail, but I knew that even if I did, at least I was living life along the way. As it turned out, not in my wildest dreams could I have imagined the life I would lead in London. I have finally got used to having confidence. The self-doubt is still there, but I use that to drive myself forward. Compared to the boy in Ireland getting beat up outside the school gates, this is a different life.

Looking back, I can see where all my hard work started to pay off. I can see why those hours spent practising on my decks ended up being so vital. I can see that, unbeknown to me, I had put in so much work before I even came to London. I can see that being bullied made me quick-witted and able to talk my way out of a corner. I can see how the discipline of training has focused me on other areas of my life, too. It all seems to have had a purpose. Yet, while it was happening, it was anything but as premeditated and neatly formed as that all sounds. Long periods of my life have been chaos, turmoil, uncertainty and anxiety. I have just kept working at it and, hopefully you'll agree that I seem to have come out the other end with something.

If someone with as little confidence as I had when I was a kid can be involved in the sort of madness that's been my life, then anyone can. Hopefully, you might see my story as an example of how a lack of self-confidence wasn't allowed to get in the way of achieving things – or at the very least, of *trying* to achieve things.

It's been breathtaking. I have had so many good times in my life, I really have. When I think about the experiences I've had, I couldn't have asked for more. So many phases have been 'the best stage ever'. I will always look to enjoy myself – maybe too much sometimes, but only because I don't want the enjoyment to stop.

I feel like I have only just started.